# The Mind Teaches the Brain

## Caleb Gattegno

Educational Solutions Worldwide Inc.

First published in 1975. Revised in 1988. Reprinted in 2010.

Copyright © 1975-2010 Educational Solutions Worldwide Inc.
Author: Caleb Gattegno
All rights reserved
ISBN 978-0-87825-064-6

Educational Solutions Inc.
2nd Floor 99 University Place, New York, N.Y. 10003-4555
www.EducationalSolutions.com

# Acknowledgements

I owe a special debt to my colleague of many years, Dr. D. E. Hinman, for doing so much for this book. As usual she takes care of so many aspects of the work that she can improve it to the point that readers enjoy much more what they hold in their hands without noticing the improvements so well blended in the work. But I can notice, and for this a big thank-you goes to her here.

Harris Dienstfrey undertook to reshape each chapter of the book in order to eliminate unnecessary material and produce a leaner text with more power. His success will serve readers and I want to thank him warmly for that.

Lisa Wood gave the printed text its final form, integrating what Harris suggested and Dee prepared for her. Obviously her good work makes this book easier to read and more pleasant to look at and for this we thank her warmly.

# Table of Contents

**Preface** .................................................................... 1

**Introduction** ............................................................ 9

    The Analytic Approach and the Fragmentation of Challenges ................................................................. 9
    Knowing, Believing, and Affectivity ..................... 11
    A Model of Man: The Learning Self ...................... 12
    Awareness and the Sciences of Man ...................... 17
    The Brain and the Study of the Whole ................. 19

**I. In the Beginning There is the Self not the Brain ..... 25**

    1 Prenatal Learnings and the Place of the Brain ............... 27
        The First Task of the Brain: To Monitor the Soma ............................................... 30
        Energy and the Functions and Structure of the Nervous System ............................................... 34
        The Coping Baby in the Womb ............................ 37
        The Integration and Subordination of the Nervous System ............................................... 39
        The Work of the Self ............................................ 42
        Other Tasks for the Brain .................................... 47
            The Body Image . ........................................... 48
            Maintaining Health ...................................... 49
            Meeting the Unknown ................................. 50
        Learning Outside the Brain ................................. 51

    The Learning Fetus .................................................... 53

2  The Function of Sleep ................................................... 57
    Challenge and the Continuity Outside the Womb:
    The Brain Learns to Monitor the Vital Functions ....... 60
    Energy and the Senses:
    The Brain Learns to Cope with Aggression ................ 63
    The Freedom and Wisdom of Sleep ............................ 65
    A Postscript on Sleep .................................................. 68

3  The Electromagnetic Self ............................................... 71
    The Self and the Faraday Cage ................................... 74
    The Non-Anatomical Grid .......................................... 77
    The "Structure" and the Work of the Grid ................. 79
    Connections to the Soma ............................................ 85
    The Brain and the Grid ............................................... 89
    How the Self Discovers Itself ...................................... 93

## II. The Brain Alone Cannot Generate a Complex Human Life .......................................... 95

4  Developing a Universe of Experience:
    The Amorous Self ........................................................ 97
    Change and Permanence in the Self ........................... 97
    Discovering the Amorous Self .................................. 100
    Exploring the Amorous Self ...................................... 103
    The Amorous Self and the Unity of the Self ............. 106

5  The Perceptive Self ....................................................... 109
    The Energy of the Self ................................................ 110

Withdrawing From Perception,
Activating Perception .................................................111

Developing Perception ................................................ 113

The Perception of Reality,
The Reality of Perception .......................................... 117

Images and the Energy of Perception .......................120

Perception and the Limits of the Mind .....................122

Perception and the act of Being ................................125

6 The Retaining Self..................................................129

Many-Sided Retention ...............................................129

Learning and Retention
in the Developing Individual.................................... 131

Retention, Remembering, Memory:
The Example of Language .........................................134

The Brain, Memory, and Truth .................................140

The Place of Recognition ...........................................144

Aspects of Retention...................................................146

7 The Intelligent Self................................................. 151

What Intelligence Does ............................................. 151

The Reach of Intelligence...........................................153

Misuses of Intelligence............................................... 155

Awareness at the Gate ...............................................159

8 The Symbolizing Self .............................................165

The Power of Recognition .........................................165

The Human Creation of Symbolism .........................168

The Power of Symbolism...........................................170

The Place of Symbolism ............................................. 172

9  The Intellectual Self ............................................................175
    The Intellect at Work:
    Learning the Mother Tongue....................................176
    The Intellect and the Algebra of Language
    and Mathematics ........................................................ 183
    The Intellect Makes the Sciences............................. 186
    The Intellect in the Whole of the Self........................ 187

## III. The Mind Always Educates the Brain .................193

10  The Sensitive Self............................................................ 195
    Sensitivity, Vulnerability, and Their Uses................. 196
    The Sensitivity of Sensitives ...................................... 199
    The Sensitivity of "Ordinaries"...................................202
    The Social Uses of Sensitivity ....................................204
    Sensitivity, the Brain,
    and the Study of Sensitivity ......................................208
    The Sensitive Self and the Unknown........................ 213

11  The Relating Self ............................................................217
    Relating to Ourselves ................................................. 219
    Relating to the Environment .....................................220
    Relating to Others .......................................................223
    The Realm of Relationship ........................................228

12  The Moral Self................................................................ 231
    The Baby and the Moral Sense ................................. 231
    Experience and the Moral Sense .............................. 235
    The Sense of Truth and the Moral Sense .................238
    Conscience and the Moral Sense ..............................239

    The Moral Realm......................................................................241

13  The Imaginative Self .................................................... 249
    Making the Potential Actual........................................ 249
    The Transforming Mind................................................251
    Imagination's Material ................................................255
    Using and Educating our Imagination......................257

14  The Aesthetic Self............................................................ 263
    The Changing Forms of Beauty................................. 263
    What is Beauty?............................................................ 265
    The Awareness of Beauty ........................................... 267
    The Thresholds of Aesthetic Feeling........................ 270
    Aesthetics and Perfection...........................................273

15  The Mystical Self ..............................................................275
    The Mystical Self in the Growing Child ................... 276
    The Mystical Self, the Brain, and the Senses ........... 279
    The Mystical State .......................................................281
    Paths to the Transcendental...................................... 282

16  The Evolving Self............................................................. 287

**Further Readings by Caleb Gattegno**....................... 299

**Acknowledgements**................................................... 301

# Preface

I do not have any of the inhibitions of scientists who feel that they must show themselves obeying "the scientific method" whenever they study any problem. Nor do I feel compelled to review all the literature and make sure that I give credit to everyone for every thought, remark, conclusion, that perhaps was written before I came upon this or that point.

My way of working is to let a challenge mold me, take the time the challenge needs to express itself through me, and integrate whatever things I have read or heard that help me understand where I am in my search of the challenge. Of course, I know that one must attribute to previous investigators what they formulated on our behalf. I also know that all this social etiquette is not essential or even of paramount importance when one is working on vital matters—and that there will be scores of critics who love the job of matching investigators and investigations and who are able to perform this job.

What matters to me is that more light be placed on a question and that the question, after I spend some time intimately related to it, tells me what to say and write.

"Some time" essentially means as long as need be, two years or forty years, or more. I prefer not to write anything until I see that I have made a breakthrough from my patient study of the matter at hand in as large a set of circumstances as is required. Since my problems are life challenges, life is my laboratory, people are the components, and what happens to them for all sorts of reasons is the stuff I look at and from which I draw <u>my</u> conclusions.

For my method to be scientific, at least to me, I must know that I am a watchdog on behalf of the world, that what I say is not said for any reason other than that I see it to be true and universally acceptable—even if I know that no one ever looked at the problem in this way and have reason to believe that no one (for the moment) is likely to agree that my proposal is worth saying.

This does not mean that I do not study some key works in the field in which I am at work, some of them examining who made what contribution and some of them the original contributions by key investigators. All the same, I am interested in making my own contribution and in writing what I think and what I have found.

* * *

*Preface*

I have never looked directly at a brain while a surgeon is operating. I have never tried to be an observer in an operating theater. My knowledge of the brain comes from books, from examining animal brains at the butchers and in the kitchen being cut and prepared as food, from books, plates, pictures, photographs, microscopic preparations, TV and many documentaries, museum and university displays. I have had a number of colleagues and friends who were biologists and spent their lives in laboratories. They never suggested that my information was grossly inadequate, apparently because what I told them seemed compatible with what they knew from their experience. This encouraged me to continue my studies, and also to read more so that I would not make any elementary errors.

Of course, I am prepared to be accepted or rejected on the basis of the facts alone. If I have not been careful enough and have drawn conclusions hastily, the scientist in me will accept getting hit on his knuckles. But if, on the contrary, I have been careful and have said only what I know to be true and can be confirmed by others, I must tell my readers that, however seemingly odd my views, a fair hearing is the only appropriate response and the only response that acknowledges the interests of all

I have written this book at an age in history that allows me to consider at length vast areas of enquiry by men and women in a number of cultures and civilizations over millennia. I am not terribly impressed by either modernity or antiquity, nor am I neglectful of the findings of any modest person who came my way. Truth has its own way of revealing itself and reaching each of us.

Intelligent observations sometimes take a form that makes them seem very unimpressive; they may sound trivial or tautological. This book is based on some observations of this sort.

The simplest of all is that since no brain has known itself and that since only minds have managed to know something of the brain, it seems futile to want to reduce all mental life to functioning's of the brain. This observation does not make the brain any the less mysterious, challenging, or important in our life. It suggests only that we may find more about the brain by knowing more about how the mind penetrates it, makes it do what it (the mind) wants, and uses it as its instrument.

The brain does not know pain while all other parts of the soma do. Does not this alone say that the brain is only a relay to the knowing self—which then experiences pain?

So much has been written on the body-mind or brain-mind relationship that students may be overwhelmed by a literature that can be interpreted in as many ways as there are attitudes towards the content of the investigations. Does not this diversity tell us that experience, not the brain, is the ultimate arbiter of truth about the subject?

It seems so strange that the mind, which knows itself so easily and in such detail, is sought in a mass of matter that is well known only geometrically, that is, histologically and anatomically. How can any one <u>convince</u> himself that some physical matter that cannot know itself can throw light on what does know itself?

Indeed, if the brain knew itself, we would not have to study it, we would be as informed about what it is and what it does as we have been for centuries about our appetites and passions—about which each living creature, and especially man, knows a lot.

Still, man can ask himself, "How can I know a part of myself, my brain, so that I know it is what it is and not something that I reach through certain awareness's?" This book is dedicated to this question, and as its title states, we start with the knower, looking at how he knows learning, and we discover that the brain is all about learning and that learning is the true scalpel, the true set of electrodes, that yields the secrets of the brain that are hidden from itself but no longer from an investigator.

* * *

In the late twenties, I began my study of the mysteries involved in the mind-matter relationship, in the existence of memory, of pain, of knowledge, and so on. I saw many ways of reaching some conclusions from these challenges but soon every one of them appeared wanting in some aspect. Rather than becoming more knowledgeable, I found myself more deeply lost in the mystery. The only plank of hope remained in my constant observation that I, like all other thinkers, was at peace in front of my ignorance and entertained only what I knew or had access to.

This led me, in the early forties, to look within my own life to enquire how I knew whatever I knew. From time to time my writings allowed me to say a few words on this in the middle of other considerations. In fact, I needed to work on everything at the same time to keep in touch with what I was all the time. I recognized myself as molecular, cellular, psychical (or behavioral), and, more specially, human four realms of being.

Because of my molecules I belonged to the cosmos, because of my cells to the living, and because of my behaviors to the animal kingdom; and as a being of the fourth realm, one who could reach the awareness of awareness, I could reach all the entries that men have said go to make up Reality.

Thus, I did not halt my quest until I knew why I slept, how I saw, how I made up my mind about anything, how I could dwell or not dwell in my appetites, my passions, my thoughts, my relationships, and so on. I realized my adherences, my endowments and endowings, my belonging to this age in my life and to other ages in it, my being in time and my making of time. I saw myself as a dreamer, a linguist, a perceiver and an actor, a transformer and a habitual being, a religious secular and a lay priest of all religions, a knower-believer, and one given to faith, hope, illusion, truth, beauty, goodness, courage, justice, intuition of the future, and activity on many planes of manifestation.

I have been granted much in this life, and most likely in previous lives. Only because all twenty-four hours of my every day have been given to life and to study, have I found it easy to be patient in front of mysteries until invited to speak of them on their behalf. I do not know any other scientific method than the one used by all those who have said something that humanity found worth retaining.

As such a scientist, I embarked upon the long route of letting what I am speak through me as soon as it was certain that by doing so I spoke for everyone of us, I spoke the truth. I now can recall an essay on memory written in the summer of 1929, as I entered the vast continent of the exact sciences, in which I suggested that memory would be understood at the same time as the brain is understood. Such intuitions must have come to many thinkers; for me, it said, "If you are interested in one, you must be interested in the other!" I believe this year is my year to put on record what I know, what has been revealed to my scrutinizing mind ready to see something else in the contemplated landscape.

This book has three parts. Part I, "In the Beginning There is the Self not the Brain," is more concerned with biological matters than the rest of the book. Part II, "The Brain Alone Cannot Generate a Complex Human Life," deals with aspects of human activity long associated with the brain, and looks at familiar questions in a new light. Part III, "The Mind Always Educates the Brain," extends the study into areas rarely associated with the brain and opens up many new questions for further study.

Caleb Gattegno

July 1974

New York City

# Introduction

Before we begin our study of the brain and the mind, we first need to examine the approach we shall take.

## The Analytic Approach and the Fragmentation of Challenges

The immense success of Descartes' method in the field of Western sciences has mesmerized most investigators leading them to become devotees of the analytic approach—which is to say, the fragmentation of challenges. So long as it was possible to produce new material in the form of laws in the exact sciences, new theorems in mathematics, new technologies and artifacts, the predominance of fragmentation as a way of study went unchallenged, and indeed may be seriously challenged today only in "frontier" investigations.

The appeal of the analytic approach has blurred the awareness that even in this approach each of us may be a system that adds to our individual enquiries the imperceptible operation of making sense, of synthesizing what has just been seen with what was already in the mind. Because of these additions, the analytic approach loses its purity—and in its purest form manages to save the day! For fragmentation alone would lead to chaos if enough researchers working in isolated corners produced findings that no one could coordinate. The institutions of learned men with instruments of dissemination in effect represent antidotes to fragmentation and opportunities for synthesizing.

Of course, if Descartes' method had been totally alien to man's ways of working, it would not have been widely adopted. If its harvest was less spectacular than the harvests of previous methods, it would not have been able to dislodge them and become the most popular way of knowing on Earth for more than three intensive centuries.

Scientists are devoted first to finding truth and only secondarily to finding it by such-or-such a method.

But scientists may become sectarian and fail to see that they maintain beliefs that go counter to their dedication to unveiling truth. That scientists have accepted the approach of being specialists does not necessarily go hand in hand with an increased watchfulness that would warn them when they move from knowing to believing.

This situation tells me that I have to watch for this shift in a scientist's mind, which makes some of his statements less trustworthy than others.

*Introduction*

# Knowing, Believing, and Affectivity

In most cases of the study of reality, there has been a tendency to work six days a week as an investigator and to return on Sunday to being a theologian, to pass from knowing to believing. Sunday work manufactured the popular line; the week's work made the esoteric line for those who read the concreteness of the world with awe and respect. These two personalities of the scientist have caused much confusion.

Our society can be divided into those who know and those who believe, and each of us, according to the day or the field, can find himself belonging to one or the other group. Most scientists have not escaped being too certain in a field of belief that did not warrant certainty, or too doubting in a field of knowledge where they could have been safe. Even great thinkers show themselves somehow capable of blurring the boundaries between knowledge and belief.

Because in the West the most socially powerful science for centuries was theology—which is still represented among us by a number of influential people—we find in our Sunday thinking the remnants of theology mixed with Cartesianism and the subsequent forms given it by Hume, Kant, and lesser philosophers. Because in the West the total person had been seen as the fallen person, some men sought dichotomies that would allow one to trust what men could find. Thus, the intellect, which was not fit to find God, was found to be fit to hold a dialogue with itself. This is the basis of Descartes' <u>tabula rasa</u> and <u>cogito</u> and, for the last three centuries, of enormous success in the world of action, so great indeed that men have almost completely forgotten the notion that they are fallen creatures and thus have relegated theology to the non-professional Sunday activity.

But because the West was also endowed with the notion of charity, it looked with a sharpened intellect at all that could be perceived in the relationship of man to man and found that in addition to intellectual relationships regulated by reason, there were political and social relationships regulated by affectivity. Almost two centuries after this perception, the West is seeing a cross-fertilization of various ways of study that give both the intellect and affectivity their rightful place. And this is done by recognizing that "affective perception" precedes "intellectual perception" in every moment of human participation, the first charging the self so that it can do the job of the intellect which then holds the charge of affectivity in check.

## A Model of Man: The Learning Self

Of all the problems confronting science, the hardest to solve has been the production of a model of man that could do justice to all the aspects of the awareness that man has of himself. Until now all the models have stressed some aspects and ignored others, leaving themselves open to legitimate criticism or bias.

Models are simplifications by their very nature, and are acceptable so long as they serve the needs of their users. The substitution of one model by another has been the perennial game of successive generations of thinkers. The question I have asked myself in this area has been: Is it possible to produce a model that integrates everything that comes and by so doing changes itself to account for whatever new perceptions adds to mankind's apprehension of reality? This requires a dynamic model, of course, one that is a function of time. And "time" does not mean only the past up to the present; we must learn to formalize or integrate the future as we have managed to integrate the past.

To pursue the question of brain and mind we need to have a portrait of the complex being in which they reside. To an exposition of this model, cast as a model of myself and my life, I devote the rest of this chapter. If the reading is heavy, it is because of the unfamiliarity of the approach. Perhaps careful reading will help bridge the gap between a linear presentation in words and the multidimensionality of the reality examined.

I not only recognize myself as consisting of four realms—the cosmic, the vegetative, the animal, the human—knowable through such disciplines as physics, chemistry, biology, sociology, theology, and psychology. I also recognize myself in time, both personal time, which involves the making and use of myself, and cosmic time, that is I have a place in the dynamics of the universe and of history.

Let us see what this means by examining the connection between knowledge and knowing.

I cannot study any question without seeing that it involves me and what I am at this moment, and that in order to respect the reality of the question I pose to myself, I have to let it reorganize myself until the question finds its place and is not reduced to what was already there. A place that transforms me.

Further, because I am in time, whenever I put a question to myself, it is a temporal question. I have to see what the question means for all the ages I have been and for myself when I have integrated all the lessons of the question.

To penetrate the reality of a question requires that the question penetrates <u>my</u> reality and that these movements between myself and the question have generated a dynamic that makes <u>me</u>. Know the question and makes the question be marked by me. If this work is continued by others after me, the question goes on transforming itself while it transforms the workers, and knowledge gains its temporal character, its capacity to be changed and renewed all the time. Knowledge and knowing are inextricably intertwined.

It is my mind that asks the questions, even if they are presented to me by someone else or by chance. Because a question, by affective definition, contains the unknown, achieving its intellectual definition is a progressive movement, and the definition is only reached at the end of the question. No question can truly be called a question unless it produces a contact with the unknown, precipitating the suspension of one's judgment and the mobilization of the self and its powers, and the respectful holding of the challenges while searching in oneself how to become ready to receive them.

## Introduction

The state of an enquirer encountering a question, which makes the enquirer into a seeker, can be called, by the affective self, intuiting the content of the question. Intellectualists distrust intuition, although they live it, cannot deny it, and need it to move towards their analysis of the question. Descartes knew it and acknowledged its existence in his intellectual work. Kant made it the "form" of one's sensibility. Is intuition more than the inevitable temporal progression in all acts of knowing? Without intuition "reason" cannot work, even if at the end of a study the watchful intellect attempts to eliminate any trace of intuition. Those who are interested only in their perception of the content of a question and not in what they or anyone does to reach knowledge, accept intuition as a weakness that needs a remedy.

If knowledge is conceived of as a byproduct of knowing and if knowing is accessible to the mind watching itself in the act of knowing, then it is possible to recast one's total life in terms of that which produces knowledge in the self, the self that lives and operates at four levels simultaneously: the physico-chemical, the biological, the psychical, and the personal. We must not attempt to reduce all knowing to only one of these levels, which is usually the approach of researchers using non-temporal models.

We are all knowers, and we all own many different kinds of knowledge, at all of our four levels. Yet we are not fragments. We are wholes. Each of us has a dynamic self that handles these many kinds of knowledge for its own ends, the ends for which knowing was invented from the beginning of time over the four realms.

In the cosmic realm and at the cosmic level, is not chemical affinity a way of knowing that belongs to atoms and molecules? Is not participation in fields of force a way of knowing for matter and energy? In the vegetative realm, are not tropisms ways of knowing for cellular organisms that function as living substance? In the animal realm, are not responses to perceptions that are compatible with instincts ways of knowing for animals which describe their behaviors?

As we pursue the meaning of knowing in man, we come to evolution.

Man simultaneously functions in the three prior realms and in a fourth, which enables him to know his knowings and thus makes him, at that level, an evolving system. Just as living things transcend matter and its dynamics by integrating these dynamics to produce the cellular universe, and just as animal behaviors transcend the cellular forms to produce all the animated forms of the animal kingdom, so man has transcended all instincts that produce species and reached the person in its unique form in every man.

In animals, evolution is in the species; in plants, it is in the forms; in the molecular universe, it is in complexity. In men it is in the individual person. Man has reached evolution. This is his evolution.

*Introduction*

## Awareness and the Sciences of Man

Man has created all the sciences. This is what knowledge is; but more, this is what "reality" is, provided we do not stop our access to it.

Because the sciences can be distinguished by man, they tell him of his many ways of knowing. And sciences are not confined only to those named today in the catalogues of all the universities put together. Perhaps every day a new science is being established by a watchful investigator who has found in himself a line of attack on something he has managed to become aware of.

The bases of the sciences are awarenesses, indeed. Man, the person, recognizes that one or more of his awarenesses has a deeper reality than he now perceives, and he pursues its presence in himself. This is not only true of mathematics, where it is obvious, but of all the exact sciences too, since laboratories are human creations to go along with the quests of men. It is also true of the social (or human) sciences, which come into being as soon as men are aware of a relationship, or a nagging challenge, that needs study.

It is also true of "the science of the whole," which can exist only in a mind as a kind of temporal pressure apart from all available knowledges and from the part of the self that holds these different knowledges as a dynamic system. What is left of the self is capable of studying the whole because awareness has the property of reaching itself.

Note that sciences are ways of knowing that men have produced from time immemorial and that these ways of knowing have become objects (in this case, sciences) by a process of the mind that objectifies them. This objectification is one of the self's ways of knowing, an important way as far as the sciences are concerned. But it does not represent all the ways that the self has of knowing. Awareness is wider than the sciences and is needed to produce their contents and their methodologies.

Awareness is clearly human. The awareness of awareness, since it exists, indicates that the self is evolving beyond the awareness of its functionings (the study of which leads to the sciences), that through the awareness of awareness the self, reaching itself and using all it has developed, can speak anew of the world, of what has escaped awareness or was too complex to be accessible or was completely hidden to a self affectively engaged in one or more layers of its manifestations.

We have to say "affectively engaged" because only affectivity provides the charge that determines the scope of a quest within which the intellect had the fun of spelling out what is perceptible. When the crops are fruitful, they keep the self affectively involved in the quest.

The self, it is true, may perceive the scope of the quest as the full extent of one's intellectual reach. Affectively deceived, one then rests in one's intellectual effort and views as a completed domain that which may be no more than an illusion of the space to be scouted. Only affectively deceived investigators can confuse their awareness of a problem with what can be known, or even needs to be known. Such confusion can make them intellectually dishonest in social situations that have nothing to do with truth.

But even if all scientists behaved in this way, glorifying their boundaries as the frontiers of knowledge and failing to be aware of what they do not attempt to know, such people can easily be surprised by someone else operating on his own. Breakthroughs have generally been achieved by means that were unknown to the occupiers of thrones and the rulers of society. They then might ignore the one who broke through but only at the social level, for "truth" speaks for itself and is capable of striking awarenesses. In all sciences, there are scores of examples.

## The Brain and the Study of the Whole

My contention is that today we can develop complex approaches akin to the complex problems that we now dare to confront and that the analytic approach has denied by virtue simply of not being interested in them. They could gain a right to be considered by analyses only if they lost the very component that made their reality—their complexity. We have been helped by the advent of the computer, itself a challenge of the kind that requires that we use ourselves differently than we have for three centuries, replacing our analytic thinking by analytic and synthetic thinking acting simultaneously, which not incidentally, we all knew how to manage in our early childhood when we learned to speak our mother tongue.

Indeed, as babies we were the kind of scientists required by "the study of the whole," we respected reality, we knew intimately all that we used in solving our problems, so often met for the first time. Because we were clear that the unknown needs to be met as itself—as unknown, we managed to do the "right" things, the proof being that out of our awareness of ourself and our energy, we objectified many uses of ourself. Learning our mother tongue and walking are two of the most obvious examples.

History has shown us men and women using themselves in very many different ways, producing different civilizations containing different cultures. But in all of them, we can see that babies have met tasks that are completely beyond the awareness of the adults and the rulers of society.

As babies, each of us has to solve a huge number of problems at the levels of the soma, of behavior, of adjustment; has to give himself the numerous skills required to survive and grow in any society; has to integrate society in himself and also transcend it. Each of us may have been distracted into accepting values that were psychologically transcendental and as a result may have surrendered functionings needed to continue the quest of self-in-the-world. But because each of us is endowed to penetrate all fields of human endeavor, this surrender may not be final, and some of us prove in our lives that it can be reversed and that the self can return to the position of commander.[*]

---

[*] See my study On Being Freer.

*Introduction*

We can learn to think in complex ways about complex things even if we have become experts in the analytic approach. These two ways of knowing contradict each other only at the behavioral level. At the personal, integrative level, they can be reconciled by becoming aspects of the self engaged in particular awarenesses.

The approach that we shall use in the study of the brain is dominated by the perspective we have been outlining. However complex the brain, it is only a part of the soma, which in turn is only a part of what is accessible to one's self contemplating itself.

Since the brain does not seem able to know itself and since it can be affected in its functions by elements from all the four realms, we shall throw some light on it whatever we explore at the physico-chemical level, the physiological level, the behavioral level, and, most importantly, the integrative level, the personal. The latter level can integrate all of the others.

While truncated and fragmented knowledge of the brain can be the outcome of such activities as surgery, drug injection, electronic surveys, and psychiatric examinations, if I want to understand man's brain, my brain, I have instruments in the self that can take care of the brain's reality in the four realms simultaneously. The literature on the brain shows a preference for truncated approaches, which have led to the view that accumulating specialized knowledge is the only way open to investigators of the brain. By taking care to account for most of the phenomena that are compatible with reality as knowable from within, we shall fertilize the studies from without and increase our insights into the brain.

I am saying that we shall be able to give the brain its rightful place in the totality of ourselves <u>precisely because we do not start with it nor end with it</u>.

As a vital organ the brain ranks below the heart, the lungs, the liver, without which we cannot even vegetate.

As a specialized organ it cannot pump blood, oxidize the blood, regulate the chemical content of the nourishing fluid. It cannot take the place of any of the organs.

Parts of the brain are not used from the start, and its evolution in an individual seems dependent on receiving properly timed signals that tell it either to make itself or play a bigger role. Its completion takes some time for each individual, thus signifying, we shall maintain, that "functions generate their organs."

All students of the brain accept the fact that, like any other organ, it needs to be treated as a tissue that consumes energy, produces waste products, and is susceptible to physico-chemical aggression and to blows from changing compositions of the blood. When we know that these operations can be dependent on emotion, one can conclude that affective life can also affect the functioning of the brain, just as we now know that the brain is involved in the expression of emotions.

*Introduction*

The question of whether the chicken or the egg came first cannot be solved on the linear frame of reference of time. Similarly, the question of whether the brain holds sway over emotion or emotion over the brain needs a complete recasting, to enable us to give each its rightful dynamic relationship to the other at different stages as required for the expression of the self.

A possible defect of any temporal model is that it makes one want to extrapolate it towards the existence of an entity at the apex and to describe Reality in terms of linear unfoldings that culminate in this entity. This requires an <u>a priori</u> ruler who knows how to organize things from the start so that each element is subordinated to the next, all the way up to the emergence of the ruler.

The observers of life in mankind, while accumulating huge quantities of observable information that can be ascertained by others, have never managed to reach one ruler who can account for all that happens in any one life.

It seems more in agreement with the accumulated experience of mankind to look upon our living as made up of numerous complex recastings by each of us of what can be recast so as to meet what is being asked of us.

Hence, we shall be doing different things at different "moments," not one and the same thing repeatedly at different moments. The word in quotes may change its meaning according to the task in hand, and in certain contexts may not mean a location on the time-axis.

And because different things need to be done at different "moments," we may need (structurally) different brains to be produced for them, or different functions of the (structurally) unique brain, if one exists.

Can we find an approach to the totality of life that will make sense to the observer who does not select his evidence to save his theory? This is what I have attempted over many years, and although I still have quite a number of important questions nagging at me and which remain outside my synthesis, a sufficient number of challenges have proved to be permeable to the light that I shall use in the next chapter, and to make sense to me in a way that the approaches of others have not.

In three publications spread over a quarter century, I have attempted to develop the use of awareness as an instrument to yield understanding of the adolescent (The Adolescent and His Will, originally written in 1949), the baby (The Universe of Babies, 1973), and of boys and girls before adolescence (Of Boys and Girls, 1975).*

Here I shall refine the presentation of this instrument and of others, and see how much more of man we can understand today because of these models.

---

\* These three titles have now been excerpted into a single volume, Know Your Children As They Are, 1988.

# I

# In the Beginning There is The Self not the Brain

# 1  Prenatal Learnings and the Place of the Brain

Like every one of my readers, I have learned a great deal in this life. Every day, now as before, I learn more. Not only do I learn, I can observe my learning. If I find that this activity of observation may have escaped me on occasions, I can enquire why. That may help me to locate the distractions that interfere with learning and remove them in myself and suggest to others that they can do it too.

I have also followed the well-beaten track of looking at a number of other people learning and as a result have found ways of improving my own learning and of making the learning by others a more conscious activity. The dual process of studying myself first and testing my findings on others, and of studying others first and transferring any learning to myself, I have used during this life.

Among my findings (a number are already expounded in my other publications), I want to select a few for this chapter.

# I
## In the Beginning There is The Self not the Brain

Learning is much much broader than the literature of today assumes. First of all, we cannot say that learning capabilities are equivalent to actualized learning. We are always much "more" than we have manifested in the circumstances of our life. A change of circumstances always solicits us anew, and we can develop what has not been actualized so far. And circumstances not only cover outside pressures. An intuition, an idea, a perception may originate an involvement of the self that mobilizes the mind as never before. Every person I meet I see as a learning system already proved effective several times over and capable of proving itself effective again and again in unsuspected areas and unfamiliar ways.

A second important set of points consists of following the perception that I use myself differently when I learn different kinds of material—mathematics, a piece of music, a new language—and asking whether it makes sense to examine what there is to learn at the various phases of my life? For example, do I use myself to learn the functionings of my soma? Or must I reserve the label "learning" for that which is visible to others? Does learning mean only what people in education want it to mean?

Of course, an extremely vague notion is not preferable to a more specific one. To see the point of broadening our grasp of learning, let us consider some of the games boys and girls play. In the literature, it has been accepted for almost one hundred years that children learn important behaviors through their games.

Since there are no official examinations to test the value of games to the players and since most of us are satisfied with what we did in those games, the question remains important only to the keen observer. Taking a beating in a fall, being hit by a rope or a ball, spending endless hours waiting to take part in a game, participating in team games and competitions, are all considered reasonable activities by the players. If there is learning in such activities, it is not in the recollection of facts or anecdotes but in the improved use of oneself, in a more shaded acquaintance with what is required and how to perform it in a swifter triggering in the mind of what is needed to cope with specific challenges. These are some of the things boys and girls learn in playing their games. Yet neither they nor anyone else may recognize that any learning has taken place.

Once it is understood that learning may leave no visible or audible track that outsiders can notice but that it instead corresponds to a change in how the self considers itself, we find a door open towards answering the question: What is there to learn at various "moments" of one's life?

Let us begin at the beginning. Specifically, is there something called embryonic, or fetal learning when we are in our mother's womb?

In my book, The Universe of Babies (1973), I wrote about what I thought this learning was, having answered first that, of course, it does exist.

Prenatal learnings provide our first perspective on the place of the brain.

## The First Task of the Brain: To Monitor the Soma

If we replace the determinism that most people blindly accept to explain the growth of the fertilized egg, positing a directed set of activities in the embryo and the fetus, we must assume the existence in each of us of an autonomous <u>self</u> that is present from the moment of conception, is unique and remains uniquely in contact with the somatic development <u>in utero</u>. This is an assumption only for other people, for in my case I cannot find a time when my self, the one writing this book, who knows itself in so many ways, could not know my soma in the way I now know it, intimately, at so many levels, responding to the subtlest change in my mind with a change in the tone of my hand and forearm muscles to produce adequate forms of the written English words. I know that this soma of mine is mine exactly as my mind is—or, rather, that both are much more than my possessions, which I can give away. I do not <u>have</u> a soma and a mind, I <u>am</u> a soma, I <u>am</u> a mind.

Both ideas of prenatal growth—predetermined development and development directed by the self—require intimacy. But the first view leaves everything to be understood while the second provides an opportunity to reach a temporal grasp of how the self gives itself a form which, in the realms of cosmic energy and of vital energy, is capable of displaying what can be molded by willed behaviors.

The self has will—or rather, will is an attribute of the self. It is present as muscle tone in the muscles that are in the soma, and it makes all the muscles accessible to the self (until such time as the self gives up its contact with a number of muscles and assigns it to another somatic agent with Which the self finds it more convenient to be in contact).

Let us notice that muscles and muscle tone are found everywhere in the soma except in the nervous system, the brain itself, the bones, the liver, and some ductless glands. Let us also notice that in the embryonic development, some tissues that will become the nervous system are as much there as are all the others and that all tissues are synthesized uniquely and solely by the embryo out of raw materials from the mother's blood. The presence of the self in the making of the soma is the guarantee that the self has given itself a form made of cells that are made of atoms and molecules (and all that goes with them) in an electromagnetic field and under the laws of matter.

What the self is learning will be objectified in the brain, specifically in the medulla and the diencephalon, through both of which the self will survey the functionings of the soma. In short, the self uses the brain to monitor the soma that the self creates.

As "vegetative life," as it is called, develops its complexities, it becomes inscribed in, is taken over by, the system of linkages that the self selects from the existing nervous system as being sufficient to do automatically what it did directly. In the two realms of energy-matter and energy-life, the self leaves to itself only the function of triggering and so becomes free for subsequent adventures. This is why the self prefers to create automatic systems maintained with the correct amounts of energy rather than remain as a constant presence in the forms that are an expression of itself. Freedom here means that the self can use what it is for what it wants to be without the burden of being taken up by the first when it is solicited by the second.

Learning at the embryonic level is displayed in three forms: in the form of the actual connections in the architecture of the soma; in the forms that belong to the nervous system and that are allocated at that stage to the task of surveying and monitoring what is in the soma; and in the contact of the self with all the connections, both directly and also through the links in the amount of brain that has been formed.

The only memory available to the embryo is the one that is inscribed in the system of linkages. That memory cannot be recalled, but it can be triggered into action on the tissues of the embryo. To inscribe the brain tissues is itself a process of organizing energy between the cells and tissues so that the presence or absence of that energy can become known to the self—which made everything with its energy and has gained intimate acquaintance with the energy left in the nerve cells.

The trillions of cells in every soma can be adequately surveyed only if trillions of links to the brain are formed. Hence the enormous number of neurons and conduits to the tissues and their concentration in central local groups to add to their capacity to draw energy swiftly from the self to mobilize the required local response. At the level of the cells during the embryonic stages, all is done in molecular terms, and the required energies are available in the very nature of the physico-chemical universe that is akin to the self at this level. The knowing self—capable of distinguishing chemicals with chemical surveyors and the physical constituents with miniaturized oscillators and amplifiers and transmitters present in the cell—operates through extremely sensitive and extremely precise procedures now known intellectually by modern molecular biologists.

For the cells, knowing is being able to distinguish the signals which say that all is well or indicate a specific sort of perturbance is taking place. Learning, at this level, is arriving at the arrangement which synthesizes all that can be kept in dynamic equilibrium and selectively (analytically) interpreting the transformations in the cells.

In the embryo, delegating the presence of the self to the nervous tissues, so that they can note physico-chemical changes in the cells, is never complete, for the self, still at work in making more organs from more tissues, will make more nervous tissues to which the existing ones will be connected. Just as the soma of today is more than the soma of yesterday, both in the number of cells and in the functions now possible, the nervous system of today is able both to relate to the new organs and their functions, and to integrate the nervous system of yesterday. The integration is done by the self itself, dwelling in the new layers of nervous tissue while it transfers to them, through new linkages, the control of the pre-existing tissues. This transforms the individual both anatomically and physiologically.

Because nervous tissues learn, there is an education of these tissues by the self. It is "self education" in the sense that the unique self is making here-and-now selections of what to transfer and where, so that functionings are maintained, work smoothly, and are monitored all the time to the satisfaction of their maker, who thereby finds himself free to get on with the opportunities open to the self in the environment, here the uterus.

Clearly, what we are talking about here applies as well to the animal realm, except that the individual animal is endowed with a species-self that teaches its nervous system to know what other members of the species have always know. In the case of man, this species limitation is transcended as soon as the individual recognizes himself as a person with a will that can transform behaviors and create new ones compatible with the soma, instead of as an organism with a soma whose purpose is to express the collective behavior of the species.

## Energy and the Functions and Structure of the Nervous System

How should we conceptualize the function of the self in the embryonic development of the nervous system as it accompanies the development of the rest of the soma? We see this function to be one of <u>educating</u> the system because its structure has to acquire the full use of the functions for which it is produced.

Now, the difference between structure and function is mainly one of states of energy. To produce structure, the molecular links must reach a certain level. This gives an appearance of a stable system, while in its interstices a continuous exchange of molecules—energy—materializes the function. In terms of energy, learning consists of adding a labile structure to the elements that were and are able to move within the more stable system of molecular links. In the neurons, such labile structures do not normally produce a stable structure nor do they leave the mobile elements as free as they were. The added energy can reach a level where a network is formed as a stationary dynamic system within a number of neurons, making available to the self all that was already there plus a new means of influencing aggregates of cells.

As time goes on, more and more complex networks are constructed with a consistency half-way between the stable structure of the tissues and the free-flowing energy that belongs to the whole self and only very temporarily is stationed in the cells. This system of networks is susceptible to change through small amounts of impulse, but the change requires a certain level of energy for it to be maintained. The system is well suited to acting as a delegate of the self in checking on the behavior of the individual cells and in sending the necessary and sufficient signals to trigger the proper action: physical or chemical at the initial stages of development, behavioral when the fetus is formed.

Automatisms—which is what this system of networks consist of—are functions which go on working without needing to report to the self. That is, they use amounts of energy that can do no

# I
## In the Beginning There is The Self not the Brain

more than trigger the involvement of more primitive layers of the nervous system. As soon as the amounts of energy required or triggered go beyond the threshold of what keeps the circuits in action, higher networks come into play. The higher they are, the easier it is to involve the whole self since at higher levels there are fewer and fewer networks to which the self has delegated energy. Consciousness of what is happening emerges when the work already done does not seem sufficient to cope with the happening in the soma or the external aggression that is causing it.

Our somatic systems are very numerous and so are their control networks. The spinal cord and the lower cerebrum are concerned with these systems and their controls. But learning, in all cases, is learning by the nervous system, because this learning is more adequate and more economical than any other, leaving all the tissues to perform the initial jobs for which the organs were created. The self knows the nervous system as its agent for surveying, monitoring, and controlling the whole somatic structure, its contents and functions.

In the early embryonic and fetal stages, it seems in keeping with the way the soma is made that enough nervous cells be produced to provide full acquaintance with all the rest of the soma. As these cells constitute new layers of the spinal cord and the diencephalon, the movement of the self towards the more recent layers generates more and more automatic functionings and therefore more and more educated cells in the brain.

All the neurons monitoring the amount of energy in the soma are affected by excessive energy shifts but not by those under a certain level. During the months of gestation, when the encephalon is generated but is not dwelled in, many phenomena generate movements of energy and as many opportunities to educate the neurons related to such movements.

## The Coping Baby in the Womb

The baby spends a few months in the mother's womb. Some of the organs, segments of the limbs, are being made during this period, but when they are completed they are not necessarily used. The liver can store reserves and can monitor and correct the composition of the blood, and the marrow can produce red cells and some defenses for the organism, but the eyes are not used, nor the lungs. The contrast between the fetus' rate of growth and the rate of diminution of the space in the mother's womb generates new experiences for the self to take care of and may lead to a specialization of some diencephalic neurons. Other experiences may arise. While DNA can store as much information as may be required to place, say, the ears and nose in their right place on the head, it cannot foresee what the mother will drink and what will be transferred to the fetus and may affect it. No one can say that the fetal world is uneventful, and the time in the fetus is solely given to the construction of the soma.

There may always be situations <u>in utero</u> when the humors of the fetus are submitted to sudden physical or chemical jolts. Since the cellular processes required to make the soma are extremely delicate, it is likely that a large number of diencephalic neurons are involved in the restoration of balance. The thalamus and hypothalamus are known to have much to do with the emotional life of man. When they are the newest layers of the nervous system, they have to cope with precisely this kind of jolting event in the fetus's life. They have to learn to recognize these emotions and to do something about them to maintain the integrity of the self, which dwells in the emotions too.

Emotions are energy coagulations lasting for a certain length of time. The state of the energy in the soma is clearly recognizable to the self since the soma is part of the self. The self can therefore educate the cells of the part of the brain that monitors emotions and can make the neurons install an alarm system which will function as soon as a certain threshold is passed. The neurons will either cause the production of chemicals to counter the effects of the coagulated energy or will cause more energy to be available to save the day.

Although there is not enough data on how the states of mothers affect the state of the babies that they carry, it is supposed that either through the blood or other devices the two are in symbiotic relationship and that they affect each other. The mother could tell us. We have to presume such a relationship for the baby or use our imagination and propose a life within the womb that seems likely.

Many questions remain. Consider the fact that prematurely-born babies have survived and in most causes have led normal lives, as if they had been born at their full term. What sort of work has the full-term fetus to do then, during, say, the last two months of his confinement? It is a long, long time. The only senses at work are the skin and the inner senses describing things as they are. They have little that is new to feed back to the self from the environment. Can it be the case that this lengthy period is being consumed with no apparent progress except in the magnitude of the organs?

In particular, the hemispheres of the brain, which will go on growing after birth, are being developed. Is there reason to assume that this time is used by the self to work on what is accessible to the hemispheres, that is, on the functional networks in the nervous system?

## The Integration and Subordination of the Nervous System

Fifty or so years ago a method of studying "chronaxy" in the nervous system was developed in France, and it led to a theory that is known by the name of integration and subordination.* It served in particular to make sense of the biological theory of evolution, which recognizes links between species and a kind of recapitulation of phylogeny in the embryonic ontogeny.

In developing this theory, experiments were performed on the length of time it took for individual nerves to react to electric shocks. The results seemed to indicate that it depended on

---

* Expounded in Part I of L'education de demain by J. E. Marcault and Th. Brosse.

whether or not the neuron of the nerve in question was in a layer of the complex medulla-encephalon connected to or disconnected from the layers "above" (called in this text "the subsequently developed layers").

Since there was an amplification of the effect when the connections were severed and an increase in the amplification when the cuts were made closer to the layer containing the neuron, the findings suggest that (1) the connections of the newest layers with older ones were not only for the purpose of transmitting signals and that (2) each new layer integrated its function with that of the one below while (3) subordinating itself to the one above.

The control of the thresholds of excitement of neurons was thus transferred from the "proper" neurons to some far away in the brain. This was demonstrated by experiments with animals and was translated into a diagnostic instrument of clinical medicine, whose findings could be verified in autopsies.

There was only one more step to take to arrive at a theory of the integration and subordination of the total nervous system—and not only to itself—and J. E. Marcault took it as a man interested in the whole of himself. But it was too big a step for other specialists working on chronaxy at the time.

Marcault made the assumption that the self was a biological entity, an assumption rejected by the scientific public of his time because of their cautious training as specialists. (Marcault did not attempt to clarify how the self gets hold of the structure that seems to have been developing on its own, as if propelled by "evolution.") He saw, as did others, that tissues and organs that at one time did not exist are at a later time present and functioning. Since a new layer of tissue in the brain seems to form itself so as to integrate and subordinate the previous layers, why not hypothesize a self, Marcault argued, that develops so that at a certain moment it becomes capable of subordinating the whole nervous system, although it (the self) is not yet objectified in a new layer of functioning cells. This would mean that the self descends on a structure only when the structure reaches a certain level of complexity and that the self takes command of only the remotest or most recent levels of a well-integrated system which ipso facto yields the whole—in short, a kind of "coup d'état" which only changes the command, leaving all as it was, in particular the functioning of the hierarchy and the institutions.*

My problem is not that I reject the self as the latest integrative schema in the somatic development, which I also hold. It is the fact that I have to account for a human embryo and fetus from the start and account for the growth of the brain in prematurely-born babies as well as in all those born after nine months. To meet my problem I invented the notion of "objectivation," which allows me to see the energy of the self organize the energy of the cosmic and vital levels found in the mother's blood and in its cells into the soma. With this perspective, there is no need any more to talk of structure being formed according to the laws of

---

* In my few meetings with Marcault 30 years ago, I expressed my problems with his model. He never said that my interpretation of embryonic growth with a self objectifying the soma appealed to him, but he said it was an even more radical stance than that taken by the East Indians!

matter as biologists see them and then, via the study of chronaxy, to assume that there are a large number of biological levels in which the last-formed level effectively integrates the previous levels and subordinates them for the discharge of its duties and that as soon as the soma is completely formed, there appears a new biological level, called the self, integrating the whole structure.

## The Work of the Self

We are contrasting models here. The most acceptable is the one capable of the greatest number of illuminations while keeping to the smallest number of assumptions (and of course is in agreement with all that so far has been established).

To own a self that is capable of, among other things, objectification—that can produce out of itself something that has distinctive attributes that distinguish it from the self but is still part of it—is to resort to an existing model where cosmic energy becomes matter via the transaction $E \rightarrow mc^2$.

While energy and matter have different appearances, the equation tells us that they are essentially interchangeable. In a nuclear explosion not all matter becomes energy that manifests itself in a number of forms (heat, radiation, blast, and so on); the explosion also leaves aggregates of matter-like particles that belong to the catalogue of classified atoms: strontium, cobalt, and others.

What happens to cosmic energy in the realm of molecules is available to molecules engaged in the formation of cells. While the precipitation of energy into matter demands very special conditions that at present are met only in nuclear laboratories, the transformation of atoms within the living seems to bypass such conditions. The evidence found in Louis Kervran's book, <u>Biological Transmutations</u>, brings us to a situation encountered a number of times when we leave the cosmic phenomena of physics and move to the biological phenomena of the living. It seems that in the billions of years of "Earthian" dynamics, there has been plenty of time to find the most economical and most efficient ways of processing telluric energy into bacteria that are capable of hosting chemical reactions—but whose man-made equivalent necessitates large man-made factories and hundreds of bright ideas and performs less efficiently. These bacteria also have ways of working, still mysterious to investigators, that in terms of energy and time very cheaply achieves what our computer industry envies but cannot comprehend.

As soon as we move from <u>in vitro</u> processes to <u>in vivo</u> processes, we can take a huge discount on expenditure and (1) manage much more for much less and (2) extend the scope of all that we encounter at the cosmic level to produce new worlds at an affordable expenditure.

Similarly, it seems that "evolution" on Earth has managed to notice that if we start with a single cell, it is possible to maintain all the effectiveness of the vital and to generate a new kingdom: the animal. Amoebae are as complex, as efficient, as bacteria, and large molecules are as complex and efficient as viruses.

## I
### In the Beginning There is The Self not the Brain

At the confluence of matter with the vital, and of the vital with the animal, most investigators attempt to apply the criteria of only one realm. Thus, we remain amazed by the fact that viruses, which are in the realm of molecules, reproduce (a function of the vital) and by what bacteria and amoebae do with the molecules of one realm to generate two other realms. These realms are superficially distinguishable by the qualities of the membranes of the cells in bacteria and amoebae, although in fact we are confronting the "simplest" samples of two amply distinguishable universes.

That "nature" places us in front of this confluence and, poetically, seems to need to start from the beginning, encourages me to bring a fourth realm to the confluence and to stress that the egg that became me was myself from that first moment on, having my <u>self</u> in it just as animality is in the amoeba and vegetablity in the bacterium.

While it is attractive to share Stanley Hall's biogenetic law, both in the evolution of all species and the evolution of a single individual, one can do without it and still account for the facts of growth. Detailed acquaintance with the molecular biological behavior of DNA and RNA brings the realm of matter to the disposal of the vital and the animal. Inscribed in the capacity to supply molecular germs with extremely small amounts of energy which will produce the large molecules of cells, all life starts anew to produce the structure of every plant and every animal. Even when the egg symbiotically seems totally dependent on the mother, it has to produce all its substance, the contents of its cells, from molecular germs found in the blood of the mother. However determined this process may seem to be to the observer, each individual produces a unique structure inhabited by the unique self that made it.

Each set of cells that form the various tissues that in turn form the various organs, is capable of using the energy of the self for the performance of its functioning. The functioning in fact keeps the structure going and justifies its presence in the soma. Thus, functioning can be taken as the most primitive molder of molecules into cells and cells into organs. When the organ has been completed, its spatial and material existence seems to impose itself more forcibly on our senses, seems to be affected primarily from outside, and becomes more "objective." For such reasons investigators (mainly in Western civilizations) have wanted to start with the structure and have attempted to extract the function from it. Fairness to truth demands that we look at the opposite possibility.

Indeed such a perspective, which assumes the existence of only observable realities such as species behaviors and personal behaviors, at once makes sense of the permanences and individualities found everywhere.

What actually evolves is something that lives and learns some individual attribute. Because an individual entity can learn through its given soma, it can affect the soma and generate changed behaviors still compatible with it, or can generate a new individual whose progeny may be a new species (which means that the behavioral change reaches the molecular scale of the soma) or can simply generate a new individual each time the entity cannot reach the soma. In the case of the human being, where the connection to the soma is both animal (when it reaches the molecular scale and transmits physical traits to its descendants) and purely human (when others isolate and adopt the function, so that selected, chosen behaviors are perpetuated in the group), we see that both biological and cultural heredity are compatible with the existing soma.

The evolution of the nervous system in the individual human being makes it possible for him to relate to his functions by knowing how to coordinate, control, and command them, and by using excessively small amounts of energy working at the "highest" (or latest) level to mobilize correspondingly small amounts of energy in the integrated-subordinate levels, the process ending up within the cells of the soma and some particular functioning. Because the self is energy, and energy knows itself in its objectified form as well as its free form, the self can simultaneously or alternately work in the various levels of the soma to maintain integrity and produce alterations.

At the same time as the self is working to delegate functions to the latest levels, it continues to supply each of the previous levels with the required impetus to keep them going.

The so-called vegetative life, which is made out of the functionings that are surveyed and monitored all the time by the diencephalon, gains some qualities that make it appear automatic. But in appearance only. For in fact, the self never totally surrenders its rights to return to any level and assess the state of things and, if need be, to intervene with a control mechanism to restore the state desired by the self at that moment.

The pituitary in the diencephalon offers a cardinal example. The pituitary is not only a part of the brain. It is also a ductless gland connected with all the other harmonic centers in the soma. Now, the two halves of the pituitary, or hypophysis, are structured in such a way that only if the brain-half issues a command will the second half enter upon its chemical course and produce selected hormones, which in turn trigger other tissues or organs to produce actions compatible with the self's assessment of the situation.

This is what we shall see at work at all stages of human growth—the self working through its control mechanisms of the brain to coordinate the growth of the soma.

In the fetal period, as the moment comes to accept the soma as it now is, completed in the sense that the tissues have become organs, the energy that is known as muscle tone responds to the self's orders to contract or expand, while the chemical plants in the marrow, the liver, the spleen, the pancreas, and other glands, only concern themselves internally with the soma and the blood.

## Other Tasks for the Brain

There still remain jobs that will require the self to use the brain in new ways.

We consider several.

**The Body Image**. First, there is the need to hold in the brain a much more easily surveyed and monitored mapping of the nerve endings that cover the inside walls of the soma. This task of the brain is not a function in the sense in which organs serve functions. It is a new job given to the brain via awareness, which is a property of the self. The bundling together of all the nerves that can send messages from the periphery through the medulla to the centers, which at once can assess what is effecting the nerve endings and can send back instructions to adjacent organs or tissues to cope with it, will produce, as soon as the self dwells in it, what we can call the <u>body image</u>. It is this which makes all of us so familiar with our soma that we can spot without error the slightest prick on our skin and go straight to the place where it happens. The body image is produced during the period <u>in utero</u> when nerves have covered all the inner surface of the soma and the soma has no new tissues or organs to add.

The body image arises in part as a result of the pressures on the skin that the fetus experiences turning in the womb and stretching its limbs. Such pressures are common occurrences of the last two months before birth. The fetus can identify each local region of the skin, and it forms in the brain a set of cells reserved for the learning that accompanies us all through <u>extra-utero</u> life as the active body image.

In my study of children's and artists' drawings, I have found this image to be a guide for those artists who work through their imagination when they produce human figures. The phenomenon of the physical mimetism of couples, who live together many years and end up looking alike, displays the reverse process, that of a mental image affecting a body image and through it the form of the soma.

**Maintaining Health.** A second job reserved for the prenatal period is to determine the "tone" of each and every organ, so that the self registers what it considers to be the correct functioning of each. This assessment then serves the self as a norm, allowing it to recognize all deviations.

Because the self objectified the soma the self knows how much energy has been locked in the physical-biological soma and how much is needed for the maintenance of the state we characterize by the word health. This means that on either side of the functioning balance—the amount of energy needed to maintain health—a deficit or an excess of energy will impede the functioning and generate a state known as disease.

As soon as the self is informed of a dysfunction through the existing nervous system, it must determine what course to take to counter it and restore the proper energy balance. The action can be a chemical process involving hormones or enzymes; it can be a biological process involving phagocytes and antibodies; it can be a physical process involving a redistribution of matter or a change in electromagnetic potential (perspiration to cool off or shivering to warm up). In all cases, a subtle and pinpointed assessment of the requirement and a prompt response characterize the functioning of the self, and this is possibly only because the intricate coordinating system of the soma has been maintained on the alert all the time during its education.

The complexity of the immense task of keeping all tissues under scrutiny all the time while the self and its somatic system are free to perform other uses seems possibly only through a system as complicated as the brain, essentially <u>ad hoc</u> yet also offering immense possibilities for meeting the unknown and the unexpected. The brain being composed of tissue must be educated and only the self can do it; the self made the brain in time, and at one stage or another it was intimately connected with the brain, determining the amount of energy to be enclosed in each new cell so that it was compatible and in harmony with the existing soma to date and with the design of a self that can do what it wants here-and-now in order to be free later to do what cannot be planned now.

**Meeting the Unknown.** In the human condition, the future and the unknown are as much guiding principles of the preparation of the self as is the use of the soma already completed in its animal, vegetable, and cosmic conditions. To prepare for the unknown means to leave open the education of the brain as well as the education of the self.

At the prenatal stages, one expression of this openness is the unfinished job of completing the brain. Since there will be a need to cope with new and unforeseen tasks, the self takes the precaution, among others, of postponing the completion of the locus of all the connections, all the means to hold together that which is more than cells and molecules, more than chemistry and physics, more even than biology.

## Learning Outside the Brain

Thus, there is plenty for the self to do <u>in utero</u> to educate itself and its brain. Yet much of its learning is outside the brain, even when this organ is connected to the learning and will somehow keep custody of it.

Although the awareness of the self <u>in utero</u> is mainly concentrated on the making of the soma and the fine structures that hold the possibility of innumerable functionings, the self is not wholly taken by this task. There are sensations that reach the self <u>in utero</u>. They can reach the blood and alert the chemical systems. They can reach to the self's contacts with the confinements of its space, bringing the skin to the attention of the self and enabling it to become aware of any impacts on the skin. They can be sensations of the regularity of the heartbeat and what can make it change, generating an awareness of time that can be connected to an awareness of the echoes of the mother's own heartbeats, with awareness of the flow of time being measured by the increase of specialized matter in the bag made from the skin. Once the flow of time is reached, it provides a frame of reference for the rest of experiencing, and it permits the location of all events: biological and psychic before and after birth; social, intellectual, and spiritual after birth.

Memory is as vivid at the prenatal stage as it will be much later in <u>extra-utero</u> adult life. It expresses itself after birth in many know-hows that look like "second nature" but in fact are first nature all the time. The self acquires those know-hows through its awareness of the edifice it has progressively made and through its capacity to use what has already been obtained to meet what comes. Later in this book, we shall study memory further. Here we can say that the subtle evocation of the flow of time that makes each of us know the soma as our own, the body image as our own, the various functionings as our own, and that warns us when some ancient structures of the soma are being disturbed, are all functionings of memory, that is, of the self attending to its past.

There are enough events <u>in utero</u> to awake the self to the existence of the non-self and make it pay attention to it so that at birth it is not wholly surprised to meet the outer world.

Clearly the coziness of the life of the womb, exalted by psychoanalysts for almost three quarters of a century because of the liquid milieu in which the embryo or the fetus finds itself, stops being the dominant sensation when the fetus cannot prevent contacts with the tightened muscles of the distended belly and the extended uterus and diaphragm of the mother. For at least two long months (a fourth of the fetus' life), the self knows that the world around it is not the wide open spaces, that it is not a world only of freedom of movement but rather one of constraints too. Learning this is another important field for the baby, and as we shall see later, it will serve future learnings.

Continuing to grow in the womb, the baby has enough tasks and new opportunities to occupy him for two months. Today, we so far are able to see that particular stretch of life—while the baby waits for the automatic hormonic upheaval that produces delivery—only in a dim light and as a confused whole.*

## The Learning Fetus

Freed from work on the actual making of its organs, the self knows other realities than the physico-chemical and biological realities so dear to the student who looks at life from the outside. These other realities may have somatic components, like the continued making of the brain, but the fetus is essentially concerned with what it can do with its experience in order to know more about the self and the self at work.

It does not take much imagination to view the fetus as being aware that its movements in the confined space of the uterus involve the umbilical cord and that this cord can become a tie and a bond rather than, as it is usually known, a path of life. To avoid being entwined in it, one must learn to cope with it. Although a loop around the neck will not choke the fetus, which does not yet use its windpipe to breathe, the fetus can perceive and assess the pressures on the skin of the neck and can use its will to extricate itself. Who can say that this has not been the lot of each of us, especially since babies are born every day with the cord in this position and some of them die at birth? We can look

---

\* Reflecting on this over ten years after the above words were written, we came to understand that the last two months are used systematically to prepare for delivery. The muscle tone of the lower limbs is brought under the command of the self, and the limbs become capable of pushing against the mother's diaphragm to trigger the hormonic machinery in the mother to prepare her for delivery.

at the unfortunate ones as those who did not learn well enough how to handle one of the hazards present in their habitat, and at the rest of us as those who learned and benefited from the experience of this hazard.

No one knows how he or she will be handled at the moment of birth. Generally roughly. But the self would not have been capable of survival—as has been the case in billions of births—if a sturdy self had not been taking care of the events to come. Even if it is possible today to obtain painless deliveries for both mother and child, we have to account for the many births that made many of us able to overcome their aftermaths and even become decent and kind people, looking for peace in human relations.

The elasticity of the fetal soma, the delayed ossification of all bones and of the skull in particular, takes care of the need to go through a narrow passage. The level of energy available in the muscle tone and posture of the fetus, so that it can use its feet against the distended diaphragm of the mother to assist delivery; the chemistry of the hormones passing between the two partners in the delivery, which makes it a joint effort and, thanks to the pinpointed precision of all the occurrences at that time, a possible one—all this may be inscribed in the genes, but it can equally well be a definite adventure of the fetus, which it wills and enters upon with awareness.

To see a self at work with swift, refined, and complex instruments, it is sufficient for us to see a baby able to appraise at each instance what he has to do and to attempt it while interpreting its feedbacks and charting his course of action because of them. The view that all this is automatic and part of heredity may not serve us equally well.

There are too many unanswered challenges in the study of life for us to be content with broad and superficial insights that leave so many mysteries hanging when a change of perspective can cast sufficient light on these mysteries for us to know their reality. The more we concentrate on studying these phenomena (by becoming aware of their existence and importance), the more we shall need adequate and, I surmise, complex instruments to come close to them. At the present time, we have myriads of isolated observations from all sorts of investigations—overwhelming evidence that new methods of work, new terms of reference, a new language to verbalize the findings adequately, can alone systematize and make them meaningful.

By selecting learning as the guiding instrument, we give ourselves the dual possibility of growing with our findings and of remaining in time. The model of the self at work objectifying itself simultaneously in the four realms, stressing at certain moments one or other of the components of its true universe, frees us from the task of having to reconcile facts that seem from outside as dissimilar as a thought and an electromagnetic signal.

In the prenatal learnings sketched in this chapter, we may have taken the easiest learnings and left the really important ones for other investigators. Clearly one man can only look at himself with what he is and what he has achieved in his successive lives.

As I write I feel that I am selecting from the <u>magma</u> of facts those that seem important to me and relate to what I have done with myself so far. I know that by doing this I may well miss what is very important to one of my readers. It will remain the job of each interested reader to contribute what his unique life has made possible for him.

# 2  The Function of Sleep

That sleep was for learning dawned on me after thirty-nine years of asking the question, "Why do I sleep so often and for so long?

I knew that I felt tired on many occasions and fell asleep then and felt rested after sleeping, sometimes only for a minute of clock time. I knew what many investigators had said of sleep, but not one convinced me that his understanding was correct; it all seemed only partially true.

When all the studies from outside seemed to require confirmation from the sleeper, it became evident that we had been on false tracks for a long time, although I appreciated all I had learned over so many years.

From outside it seems that sleepers are cut off from the world of sensation, that is, that they make use of some mechanism to shut off the responsive systems within.

For most sleepers, sleep is an end in itself; they let it do its jobs without any concern for its meaning, and they accept without any question that sleep is for rest after the fatigue of a day's work. Although such a justification can make sense for mineworkers, farmers, and people doing heavy work, it certainly does not make sense for babies nor for many people who do so little physical work.

Sleep must have some other function or functions.

It cannot belong purely to the molecular or cellular realms. No one has yet suggested that minerals sleep. In the vegetable kingdom, we can, in exceptional instances, notice sleep, which comes about from an adjustment to the presence or absence of sun rays.

In the animal kingdom, we not only find sleep as a form taken by most species, we also find that some species hibernate and extend their sleep to weeks on end.

As for men, not only have we been able to dissociate sleep from sun rays and learned to sleep under the sun and to be awake at night, we have managed to reduce sleep and sleepiness or to extend it at will in the form of total withdrawal from the world of perception.

There is no objection <u>a priori</u> to sleep having different meanings for different species or people, or even for one individual at different stages in one life. What makes us use the word sleep to cover different meanings has little to do with sleep; it simply represents one way we have developed the use of language: we occasionally change the meaning rather than invent a new word.

Sleep will be used here with two meanings. For outsiders, it will be a set of behaviors that can be described—photographed, as it were—so that most people will agree it is sleep. For the sleepers, it will be what can be reached through self-awareness. This latter meaning will let in many different things that will be linked together through the first meaning.

It is permissible that for as long as men have been aware of themselves, some sleepers have noticed when they awake that they had experienced nightmares and dreams while they slept. But so many of us rarely know we have dreamed, and have no access at all to the content of our sleep. As if something in us gave sleep a place on the clock but nowhere else. Exceptionally, people will concede that indigestion or an awkward posture may generate a bad dream.

From the outside we can notice that newborn babies sleep many more hours than they will later on. We can therefore conclude that babies <u>need</u> to sleep, without understanding what this statement means nor why babies sleep. Also from the outside we can notice that the process of waking up and of remaining awake (for longer periods as the weeks go by) is controlled solely by the baby.

If we accept that we are observing a reality that belongs to us as adults making these observations, we may also accept that we can gain an entry into sleep from the waking state as soon as we grasp what we need to explain if we want to make sense of sleep. If this happens, we will have transcended both sleep and the waking state, and have reached a more primitive entity permeating each and helping us make sense of both.

We shall reach this entity if we delve more deeply into the relationship of the self to its soma.

## Challenge and the Continuity Outside the Womb: The Brain Learns to Monitor the Vital Functions

The waking state is not a state <u>sui generis</u> to begin with. The self can choose to be present anywhere it likes in the cellular edifice it gave itself.

When the growth of the fetus and the constraints of the space containing it seem to come into conflict, the emergence into a wider space (the outer space) is triggered and takes place. Growth then neither stops nor proceeds differently. But a new set of circumstances solicit the self and receive its participation. The unfinished jobs of the prenatal period are taken care of while the self delegates part of itself to take care of the new challenges.

The baby selects to enter into a dialogue with what cannot be postponed if it is to survive in the new environment. The waking state is quickly identified with doing those (survival) jobs, while <u>sleep is a continuation of the rest of living</u>.

To use the mouth for sucking, swallowing, salivating, to emulsify the substances taken in, these functions are done at once, with the self immediately delegating them to the organs and to the proper nervous layers that are available. Similarly with breathing, linked with the air from the environment.

But once food and air are in the system, the existing functions take over and operate at the stage they were already at. To outsiders, then, the newborn baby looks asleep, while to the self it is at work learning to feel the impacts on the inner surface of the digestive parts and responding to them with what is available in the tissues and organs. The response looks chemical and specific at the various points where fats, sugar, minerals, vitamins, and so forth are passed on to the blood to merge with the functions already practiced <u>in utero</u>.

But there are new functions to be learned: how much nourishment to take from the mother's breast to keep the maintenance going and to support the economy of growth. This means learning to feel amounts, to judge the duration of the work of pumping, to improve the pumping, to undertake the ancillary jobs of breathing and eating so that they do not interfere with each other. The baby gets rid of excess by vomiting; by crying it signals that the equilibrium between the consumption of energy in the soma and the intake of food and air needs to be restored with another helping of food. To learn all this requires the self to give attention to new signals, and since the self is not the maker of the environment, it has no choice but to work on itself to meet the new challenges. These new tasks are added to the unfinished jobs, and the self manages on the whole to take them in its stride during sleep as a continuation of life in utero.

If we consider the adjustment to new circumstances as a response to an aggression on the self, aggression that requires that the self distract itself from what it knows how to do in order to acquire what it needs to survive, we can see that sleep is a return to a known integrity, to the functions that express the self to the satisfaction of a sensitive and critical self whose criteria are based on a well-grasped and well-tested reality—in fact, the criteria of a knower who is sovereign in his complex.

During sleep, the baby does all the jobs that give the new functions the stamp of all the other already accomplished functions: a thorough familiarity with them so that a portion of the brain can be devoted to constant monitoring, interpretation, control, and adaptation of what happens in them. To do this work there is no need of the environment. The self is capable of awareness at this level and of acting on the tissues and organs directly through the brain, once a part of it has been educated to take care of what is involved. Awareness starts the learning; then a continuous awareness is needed to "translate" what one encounters into what one can mobilize to cope with it. The brain's role is to take over the fine structures that have been reserved to cope adequately with actual happenings.

Accomplishing this does not guarantee an immediate and successful management of additional surprises during the waking state. Surprises test another property that the self delegated to the brain, the capacity to mobilize at once other learned adaptations of oneself to meet a spectrum of challenges.

Sometimes surprises prove fatal.

The self may have learned too narrowly how to be ready for what happens and may not have linked enough areas of the brain to be capable of summoning enough energy for the new task at hand or enough know-hows and wisdom (somatic wisdom) to decide at once how to use itself.

## Energy and the Senses: The Brain Learns to Cope with Aggression

That the self can successfully use the brain in such ways can be found in the wisdom that is shown soon after birth in the fact that the sensory nerves are not allowed to take to the brain more than the amounts of energy running along the axes of these nerves, which so far have no distracting neurons. Not until all the vital functions have been satisfactorily integrated, a few weeks after birth, does myelinization of the sensory nerves occur.

Myelinization starts the epoch of learning to look, see, listen, hear, smell, and taste, and, more specially, to know the relationships of the self, the soma, and the environment. With hearing and seeing, new "aggression" on the self takes place, requiring sleep to cope with their results.

# I
## In the Beginning There is The Self not the Brain

This is a cardinal observation of mine: not only does the brain need to be educated in the sensory field, it also has to sort out things from the inevitable aggression that vulnerability to the environment entails. So long as the self cannot choose what to do, it is submitted to aggressions. And clearly it cannot choose how much noise or light is presented to it by the surroundings. It can only choose to affect its functionings to cope with it.

In such a relation with the environment, the self has two functions to work on: one consists of not letting too great an amount of light or sound reach it by reducing the amount at the entry (closing the eyes, turning the head, cutting out the amplifying systems available); the other consists of amplifying light or sound by making available to the input some energy of the self. The self learns and accordingly educates the brain to respond in both ways; it knows what to do to the tissues in the brain so that they operate to protect what the self deems necessary at that stage.

Hence, during sleep a revision of all the mechanisms that are involved in the waking state informs the self whether it needs to retain the amounts of energy as they are in the cells of the brain, or shift them to other cells that can take the excess, or add energy to inputs that the self acknowledges are needed for emerging functionings that have not yet been sufficiently activated. During sleep a huge transfer of energy takes place in the brain—needing time, testing, and consciousness to estimate whether it has been handled adequately for the health of the complex entity of self, soma, and functionings.

The self's acquaintance with energy, which is as old as the self, and its knowledge of how to energize every somatic system, which is as old as each system and its functions, are dynamic precisely because the self has managed to monitor energy by creating many cybernetic systems on top of each structure. Hence, the self has no problem in shifting energy, in adding or subtracting energy in any of the dynamic systems it has produced to objectify its awareness of what it is encountering. This work is best done when asleep, that is, when distractions are minimized, concentration is maximal, and when continuity of acquaintance with functionings is the rule.

## The Freedom and Wisdom of Sleep

During sleep man is freer than when awake.

During sleep man can see what to do to his brain to maintain the maximum health it is capable of. Hence, during sleep the self educates the brain, to which it has no access during the waking hours when it is given over to coping with the environment and events over which it has no control.

It is during sleep that the self learns to make images. These consist of delegations of energy to the sense organs, in amounts that reactivate the paths to the neurons that inputs from the environment affected during the waking state. In the process, the self evaluates these paths and neurons in terms of the energy received, and it enhances or otherwise affects the amount to achieve control of the evocation.

## I
### *In the Beginning There is The Self not the Brain*

Because the sensory nerves were not myelinized for the first few weeks after birth, the evocations of those days were not formed as images, as they are in the following weeks, months, and years. But these evocations are of the same energetic nature and are as clearly located in the organs of digestion, elimination, and breathing (although the energy changes take place in the vegetative system) and are as clearly located and of the same nature as the earlier organs activated by still deeper layers of the brain.

We can therefore understand our brain and its functionings, as well as the organs and their functionings, as soon as we manage to reach through awareness a functioning of the self that operates both in sleep and in the waking state. One of these is the making of images.

It has been the lot of most people on Earth to study the waking state and of very few to study sleep. This has created a bias that has kept inaccessible a vast area of our experience and of our functioning as human beings.

In sleep we act directly on the subtle substance that links us directly to the three realms of the molecules, the cells, and the (animal) instincts.

This ability appears to be occasionally available to some people in certain circumstances when they are not asleep. And we treat them as exceptional because of that.

But it becomes the birthright of all of us if we extend our living to sleep and attempt to find out what we can all do when we are asleep.

Of course, in our dreams we can always perform the impossible, which tells us of the many connections in the brain that link anything to anything. The popular wisdom that advises people "to sleep on it" also tells us that we are wise when we are re-integrated, when we return to the continuum of our life where we have deposited all that we have made sense of after sorting it out, in harmony with the past and in agreement with the challenges just encountered. When we "sleep on it," we know what is our true interest, what is possible for us, what we think of "it" with the whole of the self.

In sleep we do not need the idea of ourselves that has been projected on to us by others, for we have known ourselves for months before anybody had any means of conveying to us what we should think of ourselves. And since we were then intimately connected with our soma, we had no need for exterior judgments of who we were. <u>We</u> were in harmony, even when others would later call us monsters, or deformed, or whatever they chose. Our beauty was that of functional perfection and satisfying functioning.

If we imagine that we need to return to our sources every few hours, to survey what we have become under the tests of the encounters with the lawless environment where what happens happens because of other people's wills, randomly if not altogether arbitrarily, we shall understand that the function of sleep is far more to serve our general mental health, to maintain our freedom, our truthfulness, our criteria of reality, than to dissolve some chemical poisons and make us relax.

I, for one, am sure that much of what I manage to clarify in my thinking takes place when I am deeply asleep and that when I wake up my self presents me with what only sleep could do, so that I can realize in the waking state the actions that could not be done asleep. The mutual cooperation of the two states extends overall fields of man's activity. The differences between the two states provide different forms of living, but the dweller in the two states is the same self who made the soma, the brain, and with them makes its unique destiny.

## A Postscript on Sleep

Since writing this chapter in 1975, I have continued my explorations of sleep, and I believe that I can expand on what I have written here and can also formulate my new understanding more comprehensively.

During wakefulness, the self allows outside energies to be received and held in its psychosomatic system, until the point that their integration in the pre-existing system can no longer be postponed. The self then enters the phase of sleep to continue the process of integration.

The self therefore must have two states of consciousness, one in which it relates to the outside environment and one in which it relates to its own system, constructed from the moment of conception by the law of integration and subordination. The first is experienced as <u>the state of wakefulness</u> while the second is <u>the state of sleep</u>.

Passing from one to the other is the daily routine of all of us.

Note that the self is one and that it gave itself two states that are linked only through it. The self can be in only one of the states at a time, either awake or asleep.

The awake consciousness is concerned with receiving and expending energy. The sleep consciousness is concerned with receiving a dynamic of another kind, in which the newly stored energy is handled by the already existing and stored energy, to find out how to recreate a harmony taking the new into account.

In the sleep consciousness, the present consists in weaving the fabric that was there—the past—with what has just been received over the day in the other state of consciousness.

In the state of wakefulness, most of the past is unconscious and named so; in the state of sleep, one's past and all one's experiences are the only conscious elements, the rest of the world having been shut out.

Linked by the self, the state of wakefulness and the state of sleep have done their respective jobs from the moment of birth. Therefore, later in life, we have no means to tell ourselves that we have one self and two states of consciousness, each making its contribution, every day, to our growth in awareness, to the mastery of our inner and outer world (limited to what we can reach via our developed skills), to our integrated whole.

What seems elusive in this description perhaps becomes less so if we keep in mind that by sleeping night after night and by waking up to a different environment day after day—different because it is inhabited by others who do what they do and do not repeat themselves—the only stable reality is the one we meet in our sleep, which increases by what it does rather than by what happens to one. This constant return to an inner universe constructed by ourselves in our sessions of sleep is the state of consciousness that feeds back that we are ourselves, have one experience, are well-knit and in contact with our past. We are the integrated person we are, precisely because we sleep every night.*

---

* See "Sleep Revisited," Educational Solutions Newsletter, February/April 1986.

# 3 The Electromagnetic Self

This book essentially deals with the learnings that cover everyone's life and how the brain comes to handle such learnings. This chapter examines the learning that copes with the electromagnetic field outside the mother's womb, the learning that enables the soma to adjust to the continuous changes in the field that is part of our cosmic environment.

Everyone is prepared to concede that we have to learn to adapt to our social and cultural environments, and most of us are conscious of the demands that these environments make on our effort (our will) to lead a personal life in agreement with our gifts. These demands impose an education that makes us enter the social and cultural milieu by altering our behaviors. Through such alterations, we also remain as free as we can be within the constraints of society. Knowledge of the demands is the route by which we maintain our freedom.

Everyone is also prepared to see that an education occurs in regard to the food we take from the environment to make us capable of growing somatically, maintaining our energy needs, and also having something extra, to go beyond survival. Men have the power to eat almost anything, but they have developed preferences that span a spectrum of ways of maintaining the self in the chemical energy transactions that feeding represents.

But very few people have asked about or are concerned with electromagnetic man. Recent interest in biofeedback seems an exception, but it is not really pointing at the reality and the existence of electromagnetic man; rather, it is concerned with some concomitant phenomena. Still, we cannot escape the fact that our biosphere is a melting-pot of electromagnetic fields that are separately detectable by man-made instruments such as Geiger counters, cathode-ray tubes, radio receivers, radar equipment, radio telescopes, and by such simpler tools as compasses.

The question arises of how we have managed to lead a life on Earth free of capricious interference from electromagnetic changes. Since we have managed to develop systems that can take care of heat changes, of chemical changes, and of bacterial changes, what have we done to deal with electromagnetic alterations in the environment?

The molecular nature of man is acknowledged in many awarenesses. We recognize that water is drinkable, but we shun mercury. We recognize that some growths on Earth can serve as food and others as medicine, that poisons must be eliminated (or rather, we call poisons the intakes that create an awareness that they must be got rid of as soon as possible), that we can accustom ourselves to unfamiliar chemicals such as drugs and learn to live with them—sometimes willingly.

For millennia men have resorted to herbs for medicine, and the art of preparing mixtures made doctors possible before the institutionalization of colleges. Subtle matching of herbs and conditions remains a highly respected skill of chemical healers.

For millennia it has been noticed that some individuals have ways of knowing that permit them to forecast changes in weather conditions and warn others of storms or rain to come. On my own sea voyages I knew, often twelve hours in advance, that we would hit a storm, although the surrounding conditions were calm seas and a clear sky. My stomach would feel tight. Acquaintances of mine would know through pain in their knees that the humidity in the air was moving towards greater concentrations and would forecast rain with unbelievable precision.

But the most astounding phenomenon has been utterly hidden from the world until very recently, although apparently unrelated facts of it have been known in China for two or three thousand years. I refer to the network of meridians and acupuncture points.

Because electricity is a laboratory science rather than a natural science, only when men learned how to produce some phenomena experimentally were the phenomena discovered in the behavior of cosmic entities. Self awareness had to make its way through a detour, via man's intellect and intellectual constructs.

## The Self and the Faraday Cage

Very early in the history of electrostatics, the "theorem of the electric screens" was stated as follows: "A closed conductor divides space into two electrically isolated regions so that what happens in one region has no electric effect on what happens in the other."

The discovery of this theorem permitted men to be certain that what they studied in a laboratory was not being distorted by phenomena entering from the outside. The theorem also told them how to protect buildings from lightnings and thunderbolts.

Half a century later, Faraday noted that in order to obtain the separation of space into two electrically isolated regions, we needed only a metal network to form a shield; the size of its mesh depended on the phenomena that were to be kept out of or confined to the cage that he proposed (since then known as the Faraday cage). Clerk Maxwell and his followers later refined the proposal, indicating that some of the space on either side of the wires was in fact affected by the field generated on the other side. (We must remember that Faraday was the first Westerner to become aware of fields of force and that Maxwell christened them and propagated their use in physics, thus opening the new era of electromagnetism.)

## 3 The Electromagnetic Self

Let us assume that each of us has the power to produce a shield around himself. We can say that a fetus does not need a shield since its mother's shield is sufficient to cope with outside electric perturbances.

But as soon as the baby is born, its electric systems are at once submitted to an assault from all the sources of radiation and the generators of electric fields. The self's acquaintance with the behaviors of energy must be able at once to produce the functioning that provides the most economical and effective electromagnetic shield: a shield of electronic currents sufficient to produce on the skin the equivalent of a conductor that separates the inside fields from the outer fields. Life can then go on electrically as it did <u>in utero</u>, with all systems protected.

This Faraday cage is the baby's first functional system that has no histological counterpart in the soma. It is pure function in the way that electrons are not matter but pure energy, concentrated in space and capable of establishing fields that can compose with other fields, detectable only by instruments made of materials in which electrons can flow.

Because such an electrical system has no anatomical structure, Western biologists find it difficult to accept its existence. Chinese students of man, on the other hand, have not. They did not find this system with electric probes as we now do. As observers of relationships, they noted that in many cases of neuralgia, a pressure applied to particular areas provided relief, and they engaged in an empirical and prolonged study of what has been the ancient and all-encompassing science of acupuncture.

The real problems in the field of the electromagnetic system is not whether it exists but rather:

1. Why has man given himself a grid of electron beams that move along more or less stable paths that are situated geometrically but not anatomically on the skin?

2. How does this response to the electromagnetic universe tell us about the way the self maintains itself in optimal conditions of operation on and through the soma?

3. How is this system related to the chemical and material bases of the soma through the integrative properties of the self?

4. How do the functions of the brain coordinate, or are made to coordinate with, this apparently autonomous system?

5. How does the self know itself through these various systems?

As the reader will have noticed, we do not directly consider the role of the brain until the fourth question.

## The Non-Anatomical Grid

I believe the answer to the first question — "Why has man given himself a grid of electron beams that move along more or less stable paths that are situated geometrically but not anatomically on the skin?"—is to be found at the level of modern physics that has developed the notions of energy, the electron, the field of force, and the transformation of matter into energy and conversely.

The self itself is not located in the soma like the brain or the lungs. It is found everywhere in the soma, a presence that pervades all and is in all the means found by observers: the blood and metabolism; the hormones and all the minute particles that serve as catalysts in the permanent transmutations that go on in the soma; the nervous impulses and the local electrical manifestations that are found as soon as one looks for them. From the moment of conception the self, working at the pinpointed tasks of objectifying the soma, has given itself the necessary equipment to produce the most economical and most efficient way of discharging its functions. We know today that electronic equilibrium and transmutation, and the displacement of nuclear particles, are universal behaviors in the realm of matter. The very small amounts of vital energy required to produce molecular and atomic changes make it possible for the self to maintain the extremely complex organization it must use for its acts of living. The cells may be matter, but what goes on in them is subtler and can be grasped only as movements of energy, which are known by the way they affect the instruments of the self in the self. Our comprehension of these phenomena

<u>gives</u> them their reality, and our self is better known through this comprehension.

When we say that matter always has a location, we grasp that geometry, as an attribute of the self knowing its functionings, is involved in our assertions about matter and its recognition. Locating the "Faraday cage" of the soma is as acceptable as locating the liver, so long as we know in each case how to tell ourselves where to find it.

The "Faraday cage" is known to exist in exactly the same way as the functions of all organs are known to exist—through the instruments that the self gave itself for their study and, from that evidence, through another awareness: because it makes sense to the self at all other levels.

The self cannot <u>not</u> know, at its level of molecular existence, that there is an electromagnetic universe in which it is placed and that affects its functioning just as gravity and chemistry do. To cope with the electromagnetic universe and also remain free to pursue other tasks, the self must provide itself with an integrated system that will deal with the specific job on hand and that can work automatically. This is one of the learnings of the first minutes in the world (if it has not already been done <u>in utero</u> in those cases where the mother's electric fields were not in tune with those of the fetus).

## The "Structure" and the Work of the Grid

The second question—"How does this response to the electromagnetic universe tell us about the way the self maintains itself in optimal conditions of operation on and through the soma?"—has not been studied in the West. What I can offer here is the result of about twenty-five years of examining its significance at the theoretical level\* while being involved in many different studies of learning in various contexts.

The grid I have in mind, and that I have dubbed a Faraday cage, is superposed on the set of meridians of Chinese medicine, and I have established its existence through a study of skin electricity, using a very elementary Wheatstone bridge to measure skin resistance or differences of potential. (I discuss these experiments in more detail in Chapter 10.) When I think of this grid, I hold in my mind that it exists on my skin, that it is only detectable electrically, that it is not located only in special places, that only one point on the sole of each foot can be detected by the property of a sudden drop in resistance (to 1/10 that of the surrounding points), that this point is on the fat part near the toes and still touches the ground when we lift ourselves to our toes, that there are as many such points on the head as on the whole of the rest of the skin, that the meridians, which can be traced on the skin using minimal resistance as the measure, link the points, that other transverse paths exist, completing the picture of a wired cage.

---

\* My studies on this question begin in 1951.

If electrons are channeled along these paths all the time, there must be fields that move them, and their movement must create fields. These fields could be stationary or could vary because of changing components in the electromagnetic universe.

Skin electricity is so easily demonstrated with two electrodes and a micro-ammeter that no one can doubt its existence. But very few know that it runs along specific paths from toes to armpit, and from there to the fingers on one side of the arm, and from the fingers to the neck and head, and from there down the back to the toes, closing on itself as one of several longitudinal circuits. Six circuits are on each side of the middle line of the body. On the middle line there is a unique circuit that does not go along the legs. All these circuits are electrically charged with very small amounts of energy. I do not say that their <u>function</u> is to carry these currents, only that they do and that this is observable.

Because this system exists, it serves as an electrostatic shield. But it can also perform other functions compatible with the property of being a shield. For example, it is conceivable that the micro-currents in the system envelop the soma with a variable electromagnetic field that is like the beacon of a lighthouse scanning the space around it; that according to the hour of the day, the individual currents, as well as their resultant field, are enhanced or reduced; that on the scalp, where the density is maximal, the field is more powerful and affects the electrodes used in electrical investigations of the brain, which then furnish readings attributable to the brain when they should be attributed to this system.

At the points of the grid where electric resistance is much lower than at neighboring points, the Chinese acupuncturists have developed an elaborate medical system telling us that it must be connected with the way the total energy of the self is distributed in the soma. The Chinese never considered their grid in relation to electromagnetic man, but we must. The penetration of a metal needle at these points affects the total electric balance since electrons freely move from and into the metal. Because the currents in the circuits are very small, it is possible to obtain sizable alterations of the field in them, particularly if the induced change takes place in regions where local alteration affects the overall field and at the same time provides the shielded space with selected influxes of electrons. If the needles are attached to a source of current, that is, electrons, the ease with which the current can flow into the soma through the metal reduces the protective function of the shield and places tissues and organs under additional forces that may alter the state of the inner field sufficiently to produce metabolic changes and restore to normalcy functions that were causing discomfort (disease).

But even if the needles are placed only at selected points, they can have an effect on the electromagnetic condition of the soma. Conjunctions of needles may produce a variety of impacts. Chinese acupuncturists have logged the effects of needling and have found empirically that certain constellations of impacts made by selected placings of needles produce certain restorations of functions in a number of people. They have adopted these constellations in their medical tradition.

## I
### In the Beginning There is The Self not the Brain

In the West the only all-pervading somatic systems that have been studied are the circulatory system and the nervous system. Hence, Western doctors tend to want to understand the Chinese acupuncture tradition in terms of these systems, even though the connections are hidden from them because of their way of thinking.

Electromagnetic man is as much a reality as chemical man. Moreover, the response to the electromagnetic universe can be known only when, as with the hormonal, the nervous, the chemical, and the physical systems, someone happened to become aware of it and pursued its study. The soma is the locus of simultaneous electrical phenomena, all of them fine and of short duration at the scale of molecules and cells. But when they total sufficient energy to affect the awareness of the self engaged in or distracted by other tasks, they can be noticed, and the self can return to work on the dysfunction. Acupuncture operates at the level of the small energy variations required to reach pinpointed dysfunctions in individual locations of the soma, something that drugs and a scalpel cannot do. Acupuncture is selective by its own nature, since it uses only electrons generated to affect electronic movements; on the other hand, antibodies and antibiotics bring to the soma massive material changes out of all proportion to the subtle origin of the disorder, the disease, the dysfunction.

It is a matter of model, of mode of thought above all, that distinguishes the treatment of conditions in the West and in China.

Instead of treating symptoms, acupuncturists want to restore the local balance of energy by providing minute amounts of energy at the precise place where they conceive the origin of the dysfunction to be.

They have therefore learned that health in the soma is the result of a vast number of minute balances of energy immersed in another system—the cosmic system that selectively affects the electromagnetic system of the soma and that needs to be met selectively too. Acupuncturists have found that certain hours of the day and certain environmental conditions (such as latitude, altitude, season) require changes in the placing of the needles for one and the same diagnosis of a dysfunction.

In fact, for the Chinese, functional diseases are easier to treat than organic disease, and it becomes the main job of the doctor to see to it that his clients maintain health through exercises (physical and mental) and proper nourishment and behavior. Chinese doctors very early conceived of the importance of preventive medicine, and they seem to have known what is clear to anyone holding a conception of the four realms: that the self is in command over the psyche which in turn commands the vital which in turn organizes the molecular. If the self knows itself and leads its own life, all is in order (barring accidents), but when the self surrenders its authority to a psyche pulling in many directions,* the mental disease can become a functional disease, and the soma sometimes goes haywire, leading to molecular trouble, as in the case of diseases requiring surgery.

---

\* See <u>On Becoming Freer</u>, revised edition, 1988.

Preventive medicine works best by keeping the self in command throughout life—from conception to the moment of decision that the purpose of this cosmic life has been fulfilled, and it is now time to extract oneself from its form and find a new beginning, that which we call death or rebirth.

What the self learns when it becomes aware of its electromagnetic component is that the "heavy" massive soma is permeated by an electronic soma that through ordinary electronic behaviors displays some aspect of its state and conditions. The "subtle" soma can be perceived through man-made instruments until the mind embodies the images and associates with them the clear dynamics that the intellect can generate in this human intellectual perception of the reality of fields and energy transfers. For those who can take such a route, the result is a deeper knowledge of the self at work, of a self maintaining carefully, quietly, steadily, the states of electromagnetic balance in the local phenomena accompanying the acts of living.

Acupuncture is the learned answer of the self in contact with electromagnetic man before the label was invented. It is no longer any more mysterious than is the Western approach through the brain, the approach that became the predilection of the West while it neglected the Chinese approach. I have no doubt that we can develop a Western understanding of acupuncture in terms of electromagnetism, provided that we do not superimpose on our physico-chemical model another layer called "treatment by needles" and that we do attempt to see the self in electrical equilibrium with the dynamic electromagnetic environment.

## Connections to the Soma

We turn to the third question—"How is this system related in the chemical and material bases of the soma through the integrative properties of the self?"

In all these questions we are not considering the totality of human life which we shall envisage in future chapters; we are still limiting our examination to the first post-natal learnings. Electromagnetic man is of course very close to the other vital forms as one aspect of a self that expresses itself mainly somatically.

Earlier, we brought to attention the very close connection between the self and its objectified soma seen as energy, partly locked in structures and partly free. This omnipresent free energy gives the tissues a pulsation that informs them of their subordination to a self, monitoring them through a nervous system that itself is activated by the self. It happens that many centuries ago, men found that the presence of energy in some parts of the soma could be detected in such a way as to allow to interpret the functioning of the organs with pinpointed specificity.

The most spectacular of these investigations concerned the "Chinese pulses." But it is clear to students of man that anyone who has made himself vulnerable to any one of the many manifestations of the self can proceed from his vantage point—and in so doing, can find much of value in those manifestations that are placed among the pariahs of science, such as homeopaths and occultists.

For almost a quarter of a century (since 1951) I have entertained the suggestions of Chinese medicine, not as a physician interested in cures but as someone keen to find in his mind what was needed to make sense of what he could not deny. The study of pulses (through experiments I shall consider later) must leave everyone pensive and deeply challenged. Pulses are such delicate and complex instruments that only long familiarity with them will lead to a respect for what they truly are and why they are so precious in profound diagnoses and clinical prescriptions. In this text I am concerned with what they are.

Here, in the wrist, the site of the Chinese pulses, we have a convenient part of the soma throbbing all the time with the passage of blood, between a bony platform and a thin layer of skin, offering to the touch about two inches of tissues, which, like all tissues, is inhabited by the self and its specialized objectifications of muscle tone and innervation.

Of course any arteries would do, but none are as conveniently placed or have been studied so carefully and for so long. Of course tissues other than arteries could serve as well, but again they have not suggested themselves as forcefully as the radial arteries.

Were arteries constructed of rubber or plastic, the laws of hydrodynamics would obtain, and they would reflect only the heartbeat. But they are living tissue, human substance affected by its inhabitant and by the vicissitudes of the self's functionings. From this alone we can expect that more than the heart can be detected by a sensitive observer of the artery. If it is possible for the blood to be chemically affected by some dysfunction of, say, the liver, can the blood not show to the finely-tuned tissues that receive it the cause that effected such a change? Since the blood penetrates every cell and since in every cell there are sensors functioning at the microscopic scale, must these sensors not respond to the change? And most likely do so selectively? And is the brain less informed, chemically?

The complexity of the soma has to be recognized in order to understand its extremely fine responses to local alterations in the conditions that the self maintains through the supervision exercised by the various layers of the brain. There are so many functions going on at the same time at the scale of cells, tissues, organs, groups of organs, that a proper survey of it all would completely absorb the surveyor. Hence, as we have argued, the brain is created to maintain complexity and allow the freedom of the self to meet the unknown, the uncharted, the unsuspected. Hence, the removal of consciousness from the presence of the self at every point of the soma. But not the actual presence.

It is precisely this presence that is revealed to the expert through the examination of the Chinese pulses. And it translates itself into objective properties which can be described, recorded, studied, classified, to the satisfaction of the Western scientist—and are none the less real even if he neglects them.

However remarkable we find this acute observation, made at least 2,000 years ago in China, what is more remarkable is that the pulses do indeed tell of the states of the organs and of their functions. That they can tell these things results from the omnipresence of the self in the soma; that they tell them as they do, results from the properties of the energy in the soma. If a transformation of the established dynamic equilibrium takes place anywhere in the soma, it is noted at that level by the vigilant delegates of the self. So long as the built-in safeguards can cope with it, the repair work is done in the depths of the brain layers and the perturbation may remain local. The pulse does not reveal the change. But as soon as the disturbance has reached a level requiring the involvement of other tissues or other organs, both the blood and the higher levels of the brain become part of the restoration mechanism, and even if consciousness is still not required, it may selectively involve the pulses and reveal to a careful student that something has gone wrong in a particular part of the soma in one or other of its functions. If the self is called in, because of pain or greater discomfort, its presence does not take away the property of the pulses to display the energy modifications in the soma.

For centuries acute observers among Chinese physicians noted that the dysfunctions of some specific parts of the soma followed a certain course, and they studied the etiology on the pulses at the same time as they clinically watched the whole individual. They noted symptoms; indeed, the symptoms disappeared when the dysfunction at the core was taken care of by restoring the energy balance there. For example, inflammation of the tonsils may be a symptom of a dysfunction of the intestine, and it is the intestine dysfunction that needs care rather than the throat.

This understandable way of treating patients remains totally alien to a physician whose tools for understanding reality are less all-pervasive than the self acting in every cell.

## The Brain and the Grid

We turn to the fourth question—"How do the functions of the brain coordinate, or are made to coordinate with, this apparently autonomous system?"

No doubt the Chinese have probably stuck too rigidly to their own model and have failed to discover the vast biological phenomena that Western scientists were able to find once they were aware of some appropriate way of working. The Chinese did not discover germs and the biological defenses against them, immunology; they did not develop the instruments for a thorough, detailed acquaintance with anatomy and, in particular, the brain and its very important role in life; they did not know about DNA, the hormones, and their impact upon so many human behaviors. All this they must integrate to their science of energy and in so doing make it as flexible as reality.

For the Western investigator, the importance of the existence of the Chinese way of thinking is valuable both as neglected knowledge and as a set of therapeutic techniques for cases in which Western physicians are helpless and baffled, and experience the limits of their access to reality.

Because scientist progress by becoming aware and by clearing their minds of obsolete consideration s (as well as by chance discoveries), at the present juncture we are faced above all with a crisis of understanding. The models used in various civilizations and cultures seem incapable of accommodating to each other, and men who are exposed to them feel split personalities because of their attachment to one or the other, their loyalty to their teachers, even their loyalty to truth. Hence, they waste energy in rejecting one model and affirming the other, in spite of their intimate experience that their knowledge refers to a model of reality rather than to reality itself.

Mapping the Earth on a flat surface necessarily entails distortions. It is not possible to have two-dimensional maps of the Earth that preserve all the properties that maps display on the sphere. For some purpose, one viewpoint and one method of mapping is preferable to another.

In the case of man it may well be just as impossible to account for all appearances through one model. But models are all we can produce when we want to get hold of a complex reality, and what I have attempted to do in this chapter is to find a model reconciling Chinese and Western medicine. To accomplish this, I have had to resort to a self and its objectifications in a cosmos studied by all sorts of scientists and serious investigators. What I had to synthesize were different human models of many aspects of the reality that is reachable by man's mind.

The brain, as living matter functioning in the inner space of the soma, needs to be shielded by the objectification of an electronic system that puts the self beyond the immediate aggression of the vagaries of the cosmic electromagnetic field.

The brain does not control the environment. It controls the soma on behalf of the self, which gave itself a soma and all that is needed to own it. At the level we are looking at the self and its expressions, the brain is essentially the convenient tool that the self gave itself to do a number of jobs connected with the many functionings of tissues and organs deemed vital for the maintenance of the self as a somatic being.

The brain does not do the jobs of the organs—the organs are created to do those jobs. The brain does the jobs that are intimately related to these organs; it is the surveyor, monitor, controller of the economics of energy, the messenger to higher tribunals of what is happening all the time at the levels of the cells, the tissues, the organs. By doing these tasks, it furnishes the self with the information needed to maintain the fine balance of energy at all levels.

This energy needs to be taken to precise spots in the soma, and when this happens, other organs and tissues have the opportunity to experience its passage, to become acquainted with it, and to reflect on its level and direction. The whole soma is integrated in the self, and when it is feasible, the self can take stock "symbolically" of all phenomena that go on in the soma. This is what it does when learning to interpret the states of the soma on the Chinese pulses. In so far as such learnings must be connected to the brain, the brain can be educated to know them too and to make decisions on behalf of the self. In all cases, when functions are restored without reference to a physician, the self makes use of that power delegated to the brain. For most of us, it is the most common way of maintaining our health—"leaving it to nature," as it is said.

In contrast to this capacity of the self to use the brain to work out its internal problems, the use of acupuncture is dependent upon an invention and a discovery. Unless we discover how to increase or decrease the electronic flows in particular cells, the Faraday cage is meant only to provide electromagnetic protection to the inside of the soma. The invention of needles, and the study of their impact on particular organs when used in certain ways, imposes the scale of historic time upon the very fine and local phenomena associated with living here and now. It does not detract from the fact that man as a molecular being is susceptible to molecular physical changes. Acupuncture provides these changes, and if the diagnosis is correct and the traditional observations valid, the electrons that the needles move within the soma help to restore the balance of energy at the required spots. This in turn affects the secondary transformations that are seen as symptoms of the condition and may make them disappear. This is the course of most acupuncture treatments.

But besides a correct diagnosis of the condition and knowledge of the correct set of points to prick and in what order, there is a need to know how many times the needle must be used to re-establish the balance of energy in a certain place. For the first and last phase, the physicians need a sounding-board for all the organs and functions. The Chinese gave themselves this board when they discovered that the radial arteries precisely reflect the energy condition of each organ. Through this discovery they entered the inner soma and, without having to know the brain intellectually as the West does, were able to profit from the intimate connection of the self with every part of the soma through the brain.*

## How the Self Discovers Itself

As to the fifth and last question—"How does the self know itself through these various systems?"—this question may be of importance and meaningful only to myself, but it keeps me thinking today of my original objectification of my soma and my acquaintance with the functions delegated to it. Clearly, while I am writing on this subject, I have at my disposal only what I can reach in my mind, or what my mind in the present circumstances will yield to my awareness. Clearly, because I am trying to articulate my insight and intuitions verbally, my intellect is the greater part of the mental instruments I use in writings about my insights and intuitions. Clearly, I cannot do more than these instruments permit. But because I try to focus a searchlight on what has been neglected, the light may reveal something that has not yet been known about how the self knows itself. For it seems clear to me that the almost innumerable observations of the self's reality made by man over millennia have to be accounted for if one model is to be preferred to another. The Chinese model has neglected anatomy in the sense known to the West. The West has neglected

---

\* Readers interested in a more systematic analysis of Chinese medicine and its relationship to the Western model of medicine should see Chapter 6 in my study, Who Cares About Health? (1979).

physiology in the sense known to the Chinese. But both are only aspects of the self at work knowing itself differently through either awareness.

Since today there are manifestations of the self other than those considered by physicians and scientists of natural phenomena, the self cannot be said to know itself if it manages to learn to know only its soma and functioning, even if we add the awareness of ourselves as electromagnetic beings and of ourselves as beings who echo to all that occurs in our soma.

Although learning has been extended to account for awareness of the soma and its functions, and has been considered as starting with conception, it has not yet been extended enough to take into account all that we can reasonably consider belongs to the role of learning in our life. We shall need at least all the chapters of this book to give it its due.

With the first postnatal learnings considered in this chapter we have remained in contact with a self at work on the brain which, after birth, integrates previous masteries into new powers (revealed by thousands of years of study by Chinese scholars) as the self becomes aware of a universe that was not impinging on it before but has now started its many aggressions. We shall be following in succeeding chapters, the way that our self, through awareness and its working, faces the demands of its life in a human environment.

# II

# The Brain Alone Cannot Generate a Complex Human Life

# 4 Developing a Universe of Experience: The Amorous Self

Only if we open up to the immensity of the learnings we need in order to be free to add our contribution to our world, shall we be able to take on the tasks demanded by a necessary and inevitable sequence of dialogues between the self and its inner and outer universes.

## Change and Permanence in the Self

For hundreds of years we have been brainwashed by the notion of "clear and simple," although nothing is simple and can only become clear, if ever, after thorough study. We have been plagued by conflicting models of "mind and matter" and by essentially political examinations that have purported to decide the merits and demerits of these models. The time spent in such philosophical discussions could have been better spent in studying reality and devising a method of work in which problems themselves, and not <u>a priori</u> considerations, suggest an attack to capture their meaning and significance. In such a method of work, we know what we are doing, and we do not just flail about, getting this or that insight, this or that series of unrelated facts.

The fragmentation that we experience today is the outcome of a deliberate analytic method of work in which many people have believed. But synthetic approaches, whose existence no one denies, shows that fragmentation is not the only approach to truth and reality. No one denies either that model-making is another way of knowing. Dynamic synthetic models are attempts to guarantee that the models can adapt themselves when new findings challenge the validity established by prior investigators.

When we come to the study of all-encompassing realities like the mind, the brain's functions, language, and so on, we are confronted with entities that are both permanent and changing. We have to account for the permanence in terms of change, since change is a local observation in space-time and permanence exists only when observations over a certain period uncover no evidence of change.

But it is also possible that in the field we are considering here, two awarenesses exist simultaneously: an awareness of the self, which produces a sense of permanence, and an awareness of the manifestations of the self, which produces a sense of change. Because both are awarenesses that belong to the self, the self knows that it exists (that is, is permanent) and that it also is either objectifying, or processing, or feeling, or thinking (that is, is involved in change).Today I know myself capable of such simultaneous awarenesses, and I do not see when I learned to do it if it was not at the start of this life.

In a similar manner, each of our organs has a permanence in spite of the physicochemical—biological dynamics noted by investigators, leading them to state that the content of cells is like water in the bed of a river—always moving on but stable enough within the banks of the river to be labeled permanently, "River this-or-that."

There is a sense in which we can speak of our brain, our mind, our skeleton, as permanent, and give these components an attribute, a property, recognizable only by the self. But in fact, in the space-time of experience, they are only what we perceive them to be when we perceive them. And they are always something else, because we have changed through experience or just because we do not in fact have to remain in contact with everything for more than a few moments.

In the flow of life only the knower-self has access to all that currently goes on or has gone on. If we refer, for example, to what has gone on, to memories, it is the memories themselves and not the cells of the brain that come back to awareness, even if we can prove that memories reside in cells. The self has developed ways of knowing, and these ways form the entrances to that which is known. As we said at the beginning of this book, the brain has not yet managed to know itself, yet this does not make the brain unknowable.

## II
### *The Brain Alone Cannot Generate a Complex Human Life*

In this chapter, we examine one example to explore how the self develops a <u>universe</u> of experience; how, using existing functions of the brain, it trains parts of the brain to function as knowers in that universe; and how the self comes to life in order to free itself for new tasks in this universe or in other ones.

This process is the essence of the hierarchy given in the title of this book: the <u>mind</u> teaches the brain.

The example we will consider is the "amorous self."

## Discovering the Amorous Self

One day each of us discovers the amorous self in himself. The day can be any day, but it cannot be one of the days taken up with more primitive functions, such as seeing or jumping. In the temporal hierarchies of living, the world of perception precedes the world of action, which precedes the world of feeling, of inner life.

The discovery of the amorous self happens when it happens, but not without some demands that startle the self.

Since the variety of experience is unfathomable whenever one studies a field like this, one can use only the little one knows directly or through the experience of acquaintances or through written reports.

However loving or unloving one's parents may be, the amorous self in each of us is not acknowledged until the time that the self comes to perceive love as existing by itself. One may have heard love stories, seen love films, read love magazines, even watched people engaged in expressions of love. But all this remains at the level of perception. For an individual to become part of the amorous self, it has to be activated from within, and the self must dwell in it.

Since "dwelling in" takes time and direct experience must be sifted, understood, integrated, and re-used in order to enter into further experiencing, we find that the self's study of its amorous aspect provides us with an opportunity (as do all such studies) to see how we educate ourselves and our brain for mastery and beyond.

At first it may seem that the so-called "instinct" of preservation (whatever this may mean) must be sufficient to take care of the demands of mating and reproduction. But in the case of man, love and reproduction can be separated in certain social circumstances. Today we can even assume that the current population growth must be stopped and that all couples will understand what to do to achieve this—and do it without in the least touching their love. If instincts were at work in the individual's life, one would not know about them and would not be able to interfere with them. It is much safer to approach this area with a <u>knowing self</u>, owning a will, a self capable of relating to what it experiences in order to make informed decisions.

The amorous self is not a creature of instinct; it is a product of the self examining its experience.

To put one's hand on someone else's skin takes two decisions, one by each of the parties involved. An individual may have learned on other occasions to distinguish between acceptance and refusal, but now there is something more to learn: how is the working sense of touch affected by contact with the skin, and how does the skin transmit the details of the experience to each of the people?

An individual's sense of touch has already been educated many times before. Properties like texture, resistance, wetness, and so forth, are all part of what we have learned in the world of childhood and boyhood or girlhood. So we know, when we touch someone's skin, that it has such-and-such properties, and we can use our existing education to cope with this experience, with the skin referring messages back to the self through the brain. These are the pathways we have used to prepare ourselves to meet anything from the beginning of life.

Now, we can also associate a mental or human component with the nerve inputs of touch, a component that comes from perceiving ourselves in a certain state because of the way we perceive someone else. Our perception of the someone else triggers our perception that we are in a state we may call amorous. This special mobilization of the self activates the brain through images, which in turn activate those parts of the brain that in previous stages had been directed either to release chemicals compatible with the state of the soma or to open channels that enhance the input. The amorous state must be known in its somatic as well as in its mental forms, which is why we take time to give ourselves, in silence, to caressing and to being caressed.

## Exploring the Amorous Self

What we learn varies and can range from a judgment of boredom and futility to a judgment that a universe is opening up that requires our full dedication. Until we decide to give it up or accept it as routine, the self explores the restricted or vast universe that has come one's way.

Exploration is a function of the self, not the brain. But the results of the exploration—which consists of lived experiences that take time and energy—can be left in the brain. The results then represent knowledge or know-hows, depending on how the self relates to them. Knowledge is more static and returns as images leading to comparison. Know-hows are present in the capacity to use touch to produce further consent and surrender or in the capacity to maintain the sensations of touch so as to increase their echo, to enjoy qualities that are part of the caress only when it is brought to life.

As one educates oneself to know how to use one's hand, one's fingers, to give them a lightness and a presence that agree with the sensitivity of the recipient (known through the interpretation of the response), the amorous self becomes more asserted in the self and becomes capable of commanding more of the conquered traits of the self. The amorous self in turn can become aware of the properties in it that can serve the whole self, and the amorous self may affect many of the self's attributes and functionings. But the self, which creates its own spiritual time and knows life from within, can also know that if the amorous self takes a commanding position, the self is not doing its job of being present in its consciousness and of renewing itself by renewing its consciousness.

The amorous self can decide that it is not functioning with a particular partner, and may move toward other adventures. But even when one and the same couple explore their amorous selves through each other's presence, there may be many experiences that tell one's self something it did not know—for example, something about its limitations which need to be overcome so that the amorous acts may reveal the self to itself.

Hands and caresses of the skin are sometimes the whole expression of the amorous self, sometimes only a part. Mouths and kisses provide a different challenge, and they may start an examination of whether one should advance or stop in the exploration of this universe. Contact with the sexual parts, or between the sexual parts, is again a different challenge, and is intermingled in the mind with all sorts of related or unrelated considerations that affect the working of the self.

If the self is moved by the gratification it experiences and lets go more and more, then the opportunity for learning is reduced and the experience will not educate. The experience will appear to be one in which an individual is moved by animality or allows the amorous self be used by another aspect of the self, say by an idea or an overwhelming impulse to give oneself. Little learning results from smooth functioning as usual.

Exploration is not identical with intellectual curiosity; it goes beyond such curiosity and can be utterly free of it, even though channels connect them by the mere fact of the unity of the self and the structure of the brain. But these channels are at the discretion of a self, which may or may not choose to dwell in them.

If the self is shocked by encountering the limits of its sensitivity when submitting to the expression of another self, the experience opens up new possibilities for learning more about the amorous self. If one takes up the challenge, one discovers that the self can either work on one's limits, pushing them further back and making the responses of the brain less dominant and the individual more tolerant, an education of a sort, or can acknowledge that one must seek the partner who spontaneously or otherwise respects those limits.

Because of man's complexity and the vagaries of life, there always remain uncharted areas in anyone's life. Casual encounters can reveal the self to itself, and according to the self's readiness to consider the revelation and to move itself towards the encounter, the amorous self has a future, or none, as is true for any other aspect of the self.

As a way of knowing oneself and others, the amorous self can count on a huge store of affective powers, on the fascination it seems to exercise on almost all human beings in all cultures and civilizations, on the quality called pleasure, which accompanies its manifestations in the imagination or in the sensing soma.

The amorous self is an expression of the totality of the self even when only some aspects of the amorous self are actually present in particular cases and particular circumstances.

## The Amorous Self and the Unity of the Self

We isolate the amorous self for the sake of study by the attribute of amorousness, and we distinguish it from other aspects of the self we shall isolate later on. But the distinction by which we isolate it is like a searchlight in the sky: it enhances what needs to be looked at, it does not deny existence to the rest. In fact, the soma, one's sensitivities, and one's capacity to hope, plan, express, challenge and be challenged, open up, yield, restructure attitudes, reconsider positions—are all brought by the amorous self into the life of the lover and the beloved.

One's intelligence can be fertilized because more energy is available to the amorous self for the ends of its project. One's imagination can be revamped, and the impossible seen as possible. A state of optimism is normal for the amorous self that gets a response. A feeling of doom is just as normal for an abandoned lover who has put so much of himself or herself into an unsuccessful relationship, thereby coloring <u>all</u> experiences and revealing once more the unity of the self and its capacity to dwell in its objectifications.

If one has to learn so much to be an able lover, one always learns a great deal about oneself when meeting one's limitations in the love relationships that one's life allows.

Such learnings are not thought of in connection with the brain and more often are subject matter for novels. But in our perspective, they could not take place if there was no room in the somatic form, and particularly in the brain, to free the self to meet the unknown in the universe of love.

# 5 The Perceptive Self

On the 3rd of January, 1953, in the train between Geneva and Lausanne, looking through the window at a sky with scattered clouds above the Alps covered in snow, I recovered my sense of color all at once. Rather, I recovered my awareness of colors in the world around, and I have never lost it since.

I did not know that I had lost it. At the moment of recovery I made two discoveries, one concerning my sight, which could make the world so much more attractive, and the other concerning the capacity of the self to subtract or add its presence from the functionings of the soma.

Both discoveries have served me well since. I have put color into everything I have worked on and have used it functionally. But I consider the second awareness more important for anyone wanting to understand how the mind works and how it governs the brain. For even if we know that the self objectifies the soma, we may not notice that the self must <u>continue</u> to activate functionings by supplying them with the required energy. In the complex of our functioning, there exist many combinations of enhanced and unenhanced functionings, which account for all the variety in human behaviors (without considering DNA, cultural mimetism, or inspiration, all of which can do their jobs independently).

The presence of my self in my visual perception can serve us in the study of many "exceptional behaviors" that fill the literature of the occult and the pathological, and now occupy the students of the brain.

## The Energy of the Self

In two papers published in 1954 and 1955, I suggested that since we belonged to the four realms, it was possible to develop sensitivities in any of them by enhancing our contact with the expression of the self. For example, it was possible for certain individuals to reach specific molecular impacts or specific cellular components and to develop a method of entering aspects of the outside world that most people would consider to be closed to them.

I referred to studies I had conducted of people who claimed to recognize by simple touch which of a set of unmarked bottles contained homeopathic medicines; only a person absent from the room knew which bottles contained the medicine. I was using a device that recorded energy changes, invariably my recordings indicated the presence of a change in the tracings that could come only from an alteration in the soma. The precise form of the alteration was easily readable by an expert experimenter. And the somatic change was not in the brain.

The concept behind the experiments was the idea that the free energy of the self in the soma could affect any sensitive instrument, which could pick up enough energy change anywhere in the soma to indicate it on a tracing. Since the soma throbs under all sorts of phenomena—the flow of blood, the rhythm of breathing, the passage of thoughts, feelings, conceived movements, and so on—it was easy enough to gather locally (anywhere) on a carbon microphone an input that could be converted to a tracing through a Wheatstone bridge, a current amplifier, and a recording instrument. What these tracings showed (the findings could be repeated as often as one wanted) was the direct effect of the self on the residual energy which is part of itself and is not locked in the tissues or the organs. Recordings of similar changes that I published in 1952 were already very challenging, but no theoretical foundation existed to make them believable. Now I can understand much more easily what I was recording. The theoretical basis is a part of what this text brings to readers.

## Withdrawing from Perception, Activating Perception

In this chapter we work on the component of the self connected with perception.

It is possible for the self to withdraw from the world of perception. It can as easily withdraw itself from a thought or a relationship or a worry—the last of which often happens, for example, when an unexpected visitor shows up. It is also possible for the self to do the inverse process: activate a thought, an image, or any one of the supplies of the mind that have been entrusted to a cell, in the brain or somewhere else. The process is one with which we are all familiar.

"Meditation" is a good example. So many people who never knew what it was have learned it so quickly simply because the self is expert at dwelling in its own edifice. Thus, the self can easily respond when asked to do what is given the label of meditation. And once the self makes this discovery, not only is meditation open to it but a more basic acquaintance with a fundamental expression of the self is now available for all sorts of mental exercises.

In the field of perception, it is clear that energy is brought to the somatic system from outside and that the specialized sense organs are selectively affected by photons or by mechanical impulses or by bombardments of atoms, to produce, respectively, vision, hearing, and smell and taste. The sense organs are equipped to receive the impulses. But only the self, through the brain, does the study that leads to knowing the universe of perception and to holding the knowledge for which the organs are not equipped.

In sleep (or daydreams) the will demonstrates this capacity by its ability to move energy from the brain to the sense organs, and it can give them the illusion of vision, hearing or touch, taste or smell, as a reality in the mental sense. An important property of this process is that it is free: the constraints of the outside world do not necessarily influence it. The self pursues its own interests.

Whether asleep or awake, the self can revisit its sense organs with energy that is already affected by previous visits or by visits to other senses. In the waking state this is called imagination. In sleep it is one of the functionings of free energy. Parts of the brain can as easily be affected by this internal work of the self as by the impact from outside through the sense organs.

## Developing Perception

In another place, I have suggested calling the transformations of the sense organs that occur in sleep as the result of the education that takes place from the brain to the extremities, the "functional structuring of the sense organs." The "somatic structure," given the sense organs <u>in utero</u>, makes the organs capable of transmitting outside energy to the brain. Since both the functional and the somatic structures exist and since the sleeping and waking states alternate every day, during years of practice we give our sense organs more and more education through the functions, making it possible for our eyes, say, to see more and to send back to the self through the brain more educated visions of the world, which in turn make it possible. . . , and so on.

For example, an elementary school teacher, without doing any computations in her mind, can see that some arithmetical scribbles are acceptable and others are not simply because her sight has been educated for the elements of that world. A tester can easily see whether testees are doing the right thing. An artist will know whether a distortion in a drawing or a painting is willed or accidental (and perhaps will call the first, but not the second, aesthetic).

From the moment of birth, we find ourselves in a world of lights, colors, sounds, smells, all of which change for their own reasons, outside of our control. The only way the self finds to deal with this aggression is through the control exercised by its learnings. Since it can withdraw into its bag at will and close the contacts with the world, it can dose itself with an acceptable amount of inputs and then work on them, to integrate what is significant and relevant and to store the excess energy in easily breakable molecular links or float it in the self as residual energy.

As the self first learns to cope with its vegetative functions <u>ex utero</u>, it does not permit its senses to engage in fine analyses. But once sure of the vital functions, it myelinizes the nerves and begins the thorough study of the universe of perception, the responses to it within the soma, and the dynamic acquaintance with substitutes for the transient, out-of-control, outside world. The self educates itself while educating its brain to do new jobs with the substances brought from outside.

As physicists, chemists, biologists, men can reach these processes intellectually and can assign different energy levels to the various photons, different substances to different roles in metabolism, and different functions to different tissues. But at the moment of the actual happening, the self has to deal with real energy inputs, real chemical reactions, and know how to do everything well in the here-and-now—or else.

The self must know how to cope with these phenomena at their level. This is the truth that has been blurred by the students of the phenomena. Unable to understand intellectually the complexity that the self could understand directly by working with its soma, they have made the normal miraculous and the immediately accessible sound beyond reality.

The self needs images, one of its objectivations, to understand perception, which is a form of aggression from a world beyond its control. The self can work on the energy it delegates to its images, and it can know intimately the amounts of energy needed to make the images into lasting impressions, the amounts that are insufficient, and the mechanisms that must be set up as a vigilant part of the system of the senses to remedy deficiencies, reduce excesses, or reabsorb energy altogether. In the parts of the brain to which the outside energies are channeled, there will be room for informed overseers to do definite jobs on the flows of energy that pass through them. Other overseers can be ordered to do different jobs on the energies sent centrifugally along the nerves.

Dreams and nightmares are processed in the same way. They differ only in the amounts of energy involved, which may either reach the superficial or the deep layers of the nervous system. In my study of oneiric activity, I have found the contents of nightmares to be far less significant than the amount of energy they mobilize. The vast number of dreams that leave no track whatsoever for the self to dwell on in the waking state also indicate that during sleep the self experiments with what happens when it sends its energy to activate different cells in the brain.

In relation to the inputs from the outside world, the knowing self increases its acquaintance with itself by discovering what it can do with them.

Later the self will recognize at once what certain chemicals can do to the brain, and will cooperate with them or counter their aggression, according to the point it has reached in its education. That drugs and meditation can produce similar "highs" or the same change in states of consciousness, tells us that the self can mobilize energy as easily as it attempts to cope with chemical aggression. The vividness of some dreams and nightmares that occur for no obvious reason tells us that the self, when it returns the impression of the coagulated energy in the images to the brain sensors, has the power to exalt this impression.

We have to learn so much during the time we exercise ourselves in the world of perception, that we need a number of years of watchfulness, of experimentation, of sleep, to make sense of it all and to built a substitute universe in the self in order to free it from that learning and allow it to be used. This means that we all live in an inner-outer world of constructs that we call outside reality. This "reality" can change when one of us recasts the world in a manner that makes more sense to more people, thereby leading us to acknowledge that we were not "seeing" outside reality as it "really" is.

## The Perception of Reality, the Reality of Perception

Perception betrays the perceiver at least as much as the perceived. When we realize that the brain has been in our skull for so long and that we live without perceiving it—until we place it, as we are doing here, in our skull amid the functions of a self to which we have access and in this way come to know the brain, so to say, second-hand—when we realize this, we may be prepared to say that the outside world is a projection of the self that perceives itself as perceptor.

Man is in the process of becoming to the extent that he becomes aware of what he actually does at all levels all the time. Because of his progress in consciousness, he more and more is becoming an inhabitant of a world that he is making in cooperation with the contents of the three realms (the molecular, the cellular, the behavioral) that are part of himself. Until recently he could not easily understand his place in the universe because awareness and the self were not part of his model—although no model could really exist without them.

Yet we have created models that do not acknowledge them.

There seems to be a time in everyone's life when the self loses consciousness of itself in the waking state and gets touched solely by impacts from the outside. When this happens, the self leaves to sleep the function of adapting these aggressions to what the self has already done with itself. But the task of the self in sleep has almost never been recognized. This has generated a model of the universe that is appropriate for schizophrenics, a model that the West has cultivated for over 300 years. One result is that the perception of the "outside" universe and the universe of perception are today completely separate subjects. The first is progressive because of the sciences, and the second is the object of a special science. But both deny the existence of a self, although no science can exist without awareness and although sciences evolve through the criticism of their practitioners' criticisms, a process synonymous with awareness.

Yet it is a fact that we have sciences without explicit reference to awareness and the selves who can be and are aware. It is a fact that we study perception through experiments and deliberately neglect the selves of the experimenter and the subjects.

The self makes this possible. Because the self owns awareness, it can put awareness into a contemplated object and can enhance the object to the point that the perception of it occupies the totality of consciousness.

Now, awareness of this consciousness can be sufficient to pursue the dialogue between the self and this reality. If all matters during the waking state are of this kind, there is no need to reach another awareness to cope with life-in-the-world, especially since in sleep the restoration to sanity takes place.

But all matters during the waking state are not of this kind.

The self owns an awareness of itself and of what happens to itself, but it has little to say about what happens to it in the outside. As a result, it recognizes that it makes many proper adjustments to what transcends it, and it forms in itself a set of objectifications that are reactions to the milieu and are not integrated in the self, as are the soma and its functionings. The self acknowledges these two kinds of mental structures in itself—the integrated and the unintegrated—and agrees to live a dual life: human and free in sleep, social and bound when awake. During the waking state, the world seems to be outside oneself and impinging upon oneself. Survival consists of coming to terms with the demands of this aggressor by yielding as little as one can or as much as is demanded. If such yielding dominates one's waking life, its pressures may also occupy more and more of sleep, which slowly proves insufficient to cope with it. The self that is lost to itself during sleep after being necessarily lost during the waking state, is no longer recognized as a reality. Then the world becomes mysterious to the self, thick with darkness and accessible only through continuous miracles. All phenomena are chance occurrences. Only mechanical behaviors are possible. No liberty can exist. No way out of the doom-laden downward trend of the second law of thermodynamics is possible.

We shall see later how we use our brain in the intellectual field, and how it is possible to remain in error for years. What we have seen here is how the self can manage to mistake its reactions for its own functionings, and how it can so lose contact with its creative powers, present from the moment of conception, that an individual comes to believe what the outside world (which he cannot stop continuing to re-make inwardly) seems to tell him he is. If the self no longer experiences its own functionings and movements, it becomes part of the inaccessible universe for which there is not time enough in the struggle for survival. What could have been simply perceived is ignored and is not enhanced in the self, by the self. And what can be maintained only with one's complicity—that is, by being a substitute for the content of one's consciousness—dominates one's life.

It is certain that so long as the self has access to the mechanism of its own functionings, it knows in every case what is genuine, what is true, because of the way it has operated from conception. But when confronted with the transcendental, the non-experienced, it cannot use the trusted instruments of knowing, and in its plasticity, it accepts criteria that are without roots but that nevertheless are capable of being held because of properties of the self. When ultimately confronted with what becomes accessible in due time, the self can reexamine the structure that has been produced and experience it as either worthy of integration or as needing re-structuring. Whether this is done depends on whether the will, the time, the means, are sufficient to take care of the task. In some cases, the new recognition may have immediate success, and we call its acceptance a conversion; in most cases, acceptance involves the hard job of kicking a bad habit.

## Images and the Energy of Perception

The universe of perception of course contains much more than we have attempted to describe here; it has been examined much more fully in <u>The Universe of Babies</u> (1973). Still, since we use learning in this book as the way to understand the functioning of the brain, it is appropriate to return to the analysis of the learning that is required in the field of perception, and add some insights to our education of the brain in this field.

Each sensory nerve has a part of the brain associated with it, and it is commonly held that the permanent impact of sensory impacts is found in these areas of the brain. The sense organs cut into reality and receive only selected impulses. The ear cannot see and the eye cannot hear. They are built to receive certain kinds of inputs. But the energy they let in, once in the brain, is seen as capable of passing from one part of the brain to another, thanks to special chemicals called transmitters.

In my own understanding of the work of the mind, this energy is added to the self, which dwells in all its receiving areas. Recognizing the energy as energy akin to itself, the self integrates it with itself while letting it be stored in any one of its structures—which are also objectified energy.

As the self learns to produce images by reversing the input of energy, moving it from the brain cells to the cells of the sense organs, it can send the same amount of energy to different organs and produce multidimensional images that the mind holds in itself. The energy is linked to special brain cells but always recuperable for any use of the mind, including that of restructuring the image by adding a new dimension to it.

For example, when visual images, dynamized in the muscles and even perhaps in the ears, are called to the intellect to be molded by the thought of perspective, visual imaging from then on can display perspective as an integral part of itself in the same way that color and shape earlier became absorbed into one functioning. The mind, not the brain, can evoke shape deprived of color or color deprived of shape by its use of the stress-and-ignore procedure used by the self from conception. Similarly, a scene with perspective can be altered (some may say distorted) and appear to be without it, or the mind can consider perspective <u>per se</u> without image content, as in projective analytic geometry.

## Perception and the Limits of the Mind

As readers may have noticed, in several of the sentences above we suddenly have replaced the word "self" by the word "mind." It seemed to be required by the stress on images and the functionings of the self that go with them. When the self concentrates on certain of its forms that are not already objectified by itself during its history, it may become convenient to add a term to indicate the emphasis.

Mind, like soma, is an aspect of the self—which is all it is, can be, can do. But since distinguishable aspects of self refer to different realities, they may usefully be treated separately. I can call "mind" that aspect of the self that is mainly concerned with images and their appropriate functionings. But I cannot forget, as so many do, that "mind" is merely an aspect of the self at work and that we create the mind-soma problem at the moment we accept their essential separation, although it is only a methodological device. I shall use "mind" where I would put "self" whenever it becomes easier for my readers to use this word, but I reserve the right to return to the self when this concept makes it easier to avoid pitfalls in our study, in particular to avoid being bogged down by the existence of the soma.

Since there could be no images without sense organs, that is, without the soma, there could be no mind either without a soma. Only because the self, as energy and as objectifier, can use energy to produce entities recognizable to itself, can we see in the mind a degree of lability not given to the soma (unless we reach the microscopic scale and contemplate it, as we have done, in the "local"). One of the functionings of the mind is focusing, concentration, which simultaneously produces the "local" while eliminating the rest, thereby giving the illusion that the local is the universe. This illusion, which accompanies all functionings of the mind, makes it seem distinct from the all-pervasive, omnipresent self, capable of being aware of as much of its history as it knows.

Because the mind functions as the self does, but in the circumstances of the "local," its returns are <u>sui generis</u>, and have been felt by many people to be worth pursuing. The histories of philosophy, of theology, of the sciences, are full of the successes of the mind. This has enhanced the prestige of the mind in its own eyes, particularly because it grew out of a soma that became a given, even though it produced what seemed new. The mind, so familiarly dependent on the functionings of the soma, lost sight of it, and rediscovered its existence only when attempting to look into it as "mental object"—only to find how easily it got lost. The soma cannot be grasped as images are, by concentrating on it. Its complexity <u>is</u> it, and the mind is ill-equipped to handle it.

The mind has been able to study aspects of the soma and of itself up to a point. Because the mind is analytic by definition, it needs another aspect of the self to balance its functionings and restructure its findings. The present juncture in contemporary science can be characterized as the mind reaching its limits and turning to the self for guidance. In all the sciences, the mind has reached an impasse after producing incredibly large yields. But now the glorious days are mere memories, and the challenges still loom large. The mind seeks new links with its supporter, the self, so that it can continue its work. Having tasted the forbidden fruit in attacking the "large" when it had equipped itself for the "local," and having failed to produce the "large" from the "local" (as seemed possible in mathematics through the techniques of integration), it now perceives itself as doomed only to handle smaller tasks than it feels exist.

The universe of perception now includes this perception of the mind by itself, the perception of the limitations that have resulted from the isolated evolution of an aspect of the self, which occurred because the self let itself be inspired by the open spaces of intellectual functionings. These functionings were true to the self and essentially human. Only when the self lost itself in some of its functionings, as only the free can do—exemplified again and again by those who have devoted themselves to any one of their talents—did the mind become the whole of the self in its perception of itself.

In such circumstances, the self has had to reconquer its place, its birthright, against the dominance of one of its aspects. This is happening again today but with a much greater chance of victory precisely because many scientists have acknowledged reaching the limits of the mind and have acknowledged too that their "open mindedness" means that they must return to the wider self, which contains more ways of knowing than the "scientific method." It is now possible to view man as a perceptive being with access to the four realms, perceiving in his own self the impacts from the realms and what accompanies them. In addition to the impression of light and color, he perceives photons of varying energy levels. In addition to perceiving seeing as the impact of these photons, he perceives it as the response of the brain inhabited by a discriminating self that sorts out the impacts, makes images of them, and uses them for specific ends.

Man as a perceptive being is only comprehensible if he is simultaneously taken to be molecular, cellular, mental, and spiritual. The latter integrates the preceding natures so that when matter meets matter, it is perceived as energy meeting energy that is located in particular cells, and it is manipulated to yield its messages in terms of the two-way traffic between the receiver and the emitter, so that a human life is made more abundant. All this is the spiritual meaning of perception, or more simply, the human meaning, although not all men have wanted it.

## Perception and the Act of Being

By making men part of the act of perception, we have given back a place to the soma and a place for the brain in it. If the direct stimulation of the brain through drugs or electrical currents produces phenomena of which man can be aware but which are not necessarily daily occurrences, they are potential possibilities of his being. There is still a vast discrepancy between what man is given and his restricted life in space-time, made more restrictive still by social and cultural demands on the energy of the self.

We need the whole of one life to manage some objectification of what one has perceived in it; for some objectifications, a number of lives are needed. In fact, we need the whole of past and future humanity to objectify and to sort out the possibilities of the self.

This too is part of man's perception of himself.

Looking at the sense organs and what they receive from the outside does not account for perception. Only what man does with the data makes the process perception. Some functionings are totally free of errors because they are received as an amount of energy that is added to the existing energy and are acknowledged by the self for what they are, thus nourishing the self's sense of truth; other functionings allow some trials and introduce a chance of errors, which gives the self, from the start, criteria for reviewing functionings and allows it to suspend judgment until additional evidence decides and confirms meanings. The perceiver is never passive, and his activity varies with time within the layers of awareness that form the temporal hierarchies of knowing.

When the self perceives itself in all its doings, perceives itself as the agent of its actions, thoughts, feelings, perceives itself as able to change the time of life into the time of living, the perceptive self is freed to do its work, its unique and proper work that is conditioned only by the contents of its bag and the circumstances it is in, leaving the self plenty of choice to reach the conclusion: "This is my life as I perceive it for myself for what I am and for what I was given."

# 6 The Retaining Self

A good deal of learning is thought to consist of remembering things, and many tests are aimed at determining how much of a certain amount of knowledge is retained in a student's mind. It is as if memory measured learning. Brain specialists have even attempted to find chemicals that can improve memory.

In this chapter we shall consider the workings of the self that show that a transformation takes place in the self when it has retained something of a task in which it has been engaged.

## Many-Sided Retention

It is clear that not all learning leads to knowledge—in the sense that the learning can be stated verbally and tested by questioning. If one used to be ticklish and has managed to stop being ticklish, learning has taken place, and one is different from what one was. If one used to punctuate one's speech with frequent "you know's" or "OK's" and has managed to eliminate them, one has learned something, and has become different from what one was before. Yet there is no verbal, testable knowledge in either case. Still, something has been retained, but clearly this act of retention is very different than the act of memorizing.

Since the self is engaged in the complex universe of all that it does and receives from conception onwards, it is to be expected that retention will mean different things at different stages.

The connection of nervous tissue to all the other tissues in the soma is one way for the self to retain all the functions of these tissues.

The delegation to the nervous system of monitoring and surveying the functioning of the organs, and the hierarchical arrangement of the nervous system in which the most recent layer integrates and subordinates the previous layers, are two ways of retaining control through (1) delegating what can be delegated and (2) using as little energy as possible to keep control.

The storage in the DNA of all the chemically transmutable attributes that guide the use of energy during the making of the soma is another way of showing retention (the most primitive way). DNA alone does not produce the soma. To perform its functions, it also needs all the proteins that can be synthesized from the mother's blood. DNA is a model for learning and retention, one inscribed in the wisdom of the cosmos that has had billions of years to manage the best solutions, viable solutions, to vital problems. DNA is a complex molecule, but simple compared with the brain as a whole, with the whole life of an individual and the whole course of mankind.

Since we have so many components on the Earth at the same time, we may learn something about learning and retention by looking at everything at once.

## Learning and Retention in the Developing Individual

Accidents can happen at the scale of DNA, and the guidance it provides can be faulty. A minute material ingredient can affect the whole building of the DNA edifice and produce a "monster." Retention alone is not enough to lead to an individual that can function in all milieux, for example in the social environment.

But retention is what makes heredity possible, and DNA is an agent of evolution in so far as it makes it possible to shorten by millions of years the learning done by the species on behalf of one individual.

Once this individual takes upon itself the development of this heredity, it also takes on the responsibility for all its future learnings. For months it becomes acquainted with what can be done with the basic ingredients of the DNA and the supplies from the environment, the mother's blood and the cultural influences in it.

As we briefly noted above, the individual retains access to all places in the soma and to all somatic functionings that have been prepared for birth.

After birth, the baby learns at once and soon retains all the vital functionings that are new in its new state: peristaltic movements in the digestive tube, production of digestive juices, a system of elimination that follows breathing and pumping and swallowing. The baby learns each of these functionings separately and intensely, and it moves to other challenges after educating the part of the brain concerned with each. Retention is expressed by the functioning as well as by the self's access to the organ when a dysfunction sets in. Retention is almost completely conscious but not totally. Through exercise yogis discipline themselves to reach the remnants of the self at work in the center, functionings that appear totally unconscious to the non-initiated.

Soon after the baby completes the learning of the vital functions to the satisfaction of the knowing self, learning the use of the sense organs begins. Retention, in the field of sight, is the establishment of somatic changes in the eye and the visual parts of the cortex that the self recognizes as the equivalents of the individual energy of each photon and the amount of energy input received at each moment. Another learning relates to the intensity of the input and the use of the eyelids or the turning of the head, leading to another retention that triggers the involvement of parts of the brain as soon as the impacts exceed a certain threshold of intensity.

Learning and retention also go hand in hand in the field of hearing. The sense organ analyzes the input received <u>en masse</u> by the eardrum, and sends both a spectral decomposition of the impact to the brain and a measure of the total energy received. Learning to adjust to impacts one does not control leads to a form of retention that needs reviewing again and again, and differs in listening and looking. Accordingly, the brain functions can also be different. Seeing is concerned with (1) an infinite number of impacts on the exposed retina, providing a synthetic experience which the self present in the retina acknowledges at once, and (2) the analytic action of the lens, manifested in the act of focusing, which is an expression of the will; while hearing is concerned with a blended sound that is first transmitted to the analyzer in the inner ear and only then to the acoustic region of the brain as a spectrum of sounds and intensities, resynthesized by the self in the brain. In the case of hearing, the role of the will manifests itself at the level of the outer ear, which can reduce or maximize the impact on the eardrum by turning the head.

For months and possibly for years there will be different learnings through the eyes and ears, and retention will mold itself on the kind of learning involved. For example, in the coordinations required to aim and throw a ball or a stone, what is learned is how to assess the amount of energy needed to reach a certain target or to reach the target at a certain speed. This coordinated learning must be retained, or the learner would have to begin afresh each time. The self will judge a new situation and translate it into terms that mobilize the retained ability. Hence the possibility of errors in such events.

## Retention, Remembering, Memory: The Example of Language

No one can say that he "remembers" such activities although he retains them. We shall use "remember" in an exclusive sense. Retention of what we cannot provide for ourselves, invent from out of our own equipment, we shall consider needs to be remembered. Remembering is required in many cases but not in the fields of perception, action, feelings, thinking, and the like. In a case where remembering is required, retention is also functioning, but not necessarily the other way around.

Memory, as the objectification of retention, will therefore show two very different functionings according to whether remembering (as we define it) is present or not. Retention, being a function of the self, can become unconscious to the extent that the self delegates it to deeper layers of its structure. But remembering, not being necessary for survival in the cosmos, can be forgotten or lost to the self because the additional energy associated with the item to be remembered may not be sufficient to ensure integration in the self.

In sleep we undertake the study of the energies mobilized by remembering, and we retain what seems vital to the self and recuperate the insufficient energy loaned to a memory track. We also fortify some of these delegations of energy in sleep and wake up remembering more than when we went to sleep.

In my pedagogical work I have introduced the notion of an "ogden," the unit of energy needed to remember and retain any alien item. Unless the ogdens have been paid, there is no place for these aliens in one's memory. Students in school often refuse to pay ogdens for the facts of arithmetic when they are presented as things to be remembered. (Actually, these facts can easily be retained if they are presented functionally. See my brief discussion in Chapter 14 of <u>On Being Freer</u>.)

Having made these distinctions, we can now attempt to understand memory as a function of the self and to understand the place of memory in growth and learning. A good example to work on is language. It requires retention, and since vocabulary cannot be invented, it needs to be remembered. But no native speaker can be said to remember his language since it has become a functioning of his self.

The basic awareness babies have in the field of language is of themselves as uttering systems. Hearing babies can hear each of their own utterances. Deaf babies soon abandon the study of the voluntary mobilization of their phonic apparatus.

Babies have a dual awareness of their production of sounds: one awareness arises by knowing directly how to produce utterances by using their lungs, larynx, tongue and lips, and then attempting to reproduce the conditions; the other awareness arises from the impact upon their ears of these utterances, which babies can know as outside impacts. Using these two systems separately for a while, babies come to link a willed functioning (in which awareness is necessarily present) and a passive reception of impacts on the eardrum, which they analyze like all others. Once they understand that what they hear is caused by what they utter, they own two very different systems that the self organizes into a living unity. The part of the brain

involved in the world of sound can now decode its own muscular energizing. This permits the transfer of successive and separate moves of the self into the more permanent substance of brain-cell changes, and the moves can all be surveyed at the same time instead of in the temporal sequence of the utterances. The brain is now aware of the qualities that characterize the tissues in the mouth and form the timbre of the voice, and aware also of the intensity of the utterances, measured in the usual energy units which connect the value of the variable sound produced by the air passing through the vocal cords to the amount of air expelled through the larynx, so that each sound can be produced or reproduced by a configuration that the self knows directly because it wills it.

Each impact of these successive utterances upon the ear is analyzed by and sent to the brain, so that what remains constant is recognized as such (it concerns mainly the timbre) and what is variable is associated with a spectrum of latitudes that may include intensity.

The self can now use in reverse this material that is stored in the brain. It can generate vocal images in the ear and the throat by sending its energy back into the inner ear and throat. It will continue to do this until the self knows that the inscriptions in the brain are sufficient to trigger all that has been inscribed. The potential dynamic structure is now as good as the experience, and the self is free to explore ahead.

## 6 The Retaining Self

What is retained is the quality of the voice and its spectrum as well as the actual utterances of which the baby is capable. There is nothing so far to remember.

As the spectrum of utterances widens, one day someone in the environment notices that an utterance of the baby resembles an utterance that the environment associates with a perception that gives the utterance what is called its meaning, and the bridge between the ability of the baby to utter and of the environment to speak has been formed. From now on, some of the attention of the baby will go to the utterances of his family, who suddenly repeat what he utters, giving him a new stream of sounds to work on and to connect with his stored material. Again, there is still no need to remember, for he hears in their imitation only what he knows.

But as soon as he decides to pick up something that he hears (and analyzes in terms of his own utterances), he becomes dependent for his judgment of rightness upon <u>their</u> acceptance. He can trust his hearing and the system that links it to his utterance system. But now the sounds he hears and utters are connected to him in an entirely mysterious manner, to what he may perceive or not. If he does, he can guess the connection, and can use his intelligence to form a third system connected with hearing and uttering, that is, by evoking some image, feeling, movement, or anything else. The brain will now produce the links, and the baby will pay an "ogden" to establish a connection between the image and whatever utterance he has decided represents what he heard.

What the baby now has to remember is a non-necessary connection. The rest is the usage of existing functionings triggered at no cost by the will. Errors in utterance are corrected by the existing system, not the baby's parents, and only an awareness of discrepancies between what he hears himself utter and what he hears others utter will trigger the desire to change his objectification.

As the self pays the necessary ogdens for the elements the self wishes to remember and finds how to use, the payment of ogdens becomes a functioning of the self, and the repeated usage of the retained utterances produces a triggering system that gives the self's memory of the language the characteristics of a functioning. When this happens, one no longer knows that the native language was learned by paying ogdens. This will also be the case with any new "foreign" language.

In one's memory we not only find the objectifications that produced the words of the language but also the dynamics that go with the energy mobilized for them. We no longer notice that ogdens have been paid, one for every word, but we do notice that we have had to attend to many accompanying components. Stress on words, intonation, breathing, emotions, the melody of a statement—each of them has to make its impact in terms of energy (or in terms of the distribution of energy along the time coordinate), until in our rendering of the utterance of the retained words, we discover the significance of each and of all.

No ogdens are needed for these components of expression: the plasticity of the brain allows them to affect cells in groups so that the evocation of meaning results partly from the ogdens paid and partly from the energized grouping. Thus, "it is" and "is it" use the same two ogdens, but the energy differs for each pair, and the self acknowledges the difference by evoking two states connected with the energies in the voice. Later, when a sufficient number of strings of utterances exist, the self can recognize that the energies associated with variable ogdens have something in common and that the trend distinguishes, for example, questions or doubts from affirmations. No ogdens are paid for this discovery, for there is nothing to remember.

In the case of words that are not used again and again, it is possible that the payment of ogdens will not be effective and that forgetting will occur. Babies soon find out which words in the environment's vocabulary are more useful in expressing what they want to share with others, and babies concentrate on these words, obtaining the impression that their usage establishes the easy availability of all words. Still, babies learn thousands of words in three or four years just by learning words that correspond to meanings they already have access to. These meanings trigger the words, and the words trigger the meanings. Soon words and meanings are interchangeable.

Words nevertheless have functions, and these have to become clear to any one before he can use them as native speakers do. No ogdens are required for these functions since one only needs to observe how the order of words or some special words affect meaning. After testing the observations on the environment, the findings are adopted. Babies notice that one ogden for the word "he" is sufficient to replace many ogdens for the names of all the male people around and to come. A baby recognizes the existence of perceptible attributes, and they form themselves in his mind, and through that a specific set of connections forms in his brain which can trigger pronouns for nouns and conversely.

## The Brain, Memory, and Truth

The brain cannot do such a thing for itself and needs to be "educated" to do it with immediacy, automatically.

Hence, the retaining self operates within the self that fills both the interstices of the brain and the cells that produce millions of chemical reactions corresponding to millions of energy exchanges. The mind by itself can see chemical reactions, and can see they serve the purpose of retention. As we said earlier, the appearance of permanence is in reality a stationary dynamics in which what is exchanged counts for balance rather than actual change. Since images are coagulated energy and since the energy that has been given by the self is linked to the non-structured self (in other words, is free energy), the functioning of memory must belong to the non-structured self. Through these dynamic links, images can be recalled or moved out of the focal point of the mind. The mind owns the power of concentration and relaxation, and through these powers some content can become more illuminated than another content or can vanish into the organized structure of the brain. Since it is energy that is displaced, this movement could be a movement of atoms (hence chemical reactions) as easily as a movement of electrical currents (or electrons, which are also found in atoms). At the scale of these dynamics, it may well be that both descriptions are acceptable (as the Principle of Complementarity in quantum mechanics has made two models of atomic reality acceptable).

In the brain, memory is nothing if it is not perceived as dynamic and not seen in its reality, that is, with all the components of holding, releasing, eliminating. No one can think of memory without considering forgetting. We all feel right when we remember something but astonished that such-or-such a thing is forgotten. We know ourselves as capable of retention, of retaining a great deal, and we consider forgetting what we once knew as a dysfunction. The truth is that we each have developed ways of penetrating the given with our mind. We each perceive discriminately, perceiving and giving mental energy to a component of the perception so that it can be activated into significance. But at the same time that this discrimination provides something retained, it provides for something left out, ignored, neglected. Our brain is educated to be selective of memories as a matter of course. It is not possible to uniformize memory by the device of exposing many people to the same event, talk, demonstration, because exposure is only one component of the act. The individual's life, biases, interests of the moment, degree of participation, insights into the matter, and so forth, create the unique, different, individual, final product.

Even when the given is a poem or a song, say, it is the elements that intertwine with the deliberate maintenance of the original words or notes to produce the true unique delivery. The public listening to a song <u>seems</u> to be in agreement about a rendering because what is stressed <u>seems</u> to be the same for all the participants. But here too the process takes care of variations by ignoring them or their significance.

When we consider collective memory or the memory of a computer, we have to drop some important components of the first type of memory and generate a notion of uniformity that reduces the true function to a schema (exemplified in the computer by magnetic inscription on a magnetic tape) whose main property is fidelity.

In the oral transmission of the wisdom and traditions of a tribe from generation to generation, education for fidelity was possible by means of a compromise between those who carried the lessons: one watched how the individuals transformed the given and countered the process to the satisfaction of others. From such acquired discipline came the demands of instructors in teaching institutions that students spend their time forcing their memory to be faithful, rather than to function as it normally does in day-to-day living, stressing some components and ignoring others on an individual basis.

We associate ourselves with the collective memory—best demonstrated today in the stored material found in libraries of books, films, or tapes—through a process of linking to it rather than through the fidelity of our own memory, which we allow to function individually through interpretation, criticism, expansion, correction, cross-reference—all the components that are part of our mind's view of our memory.

In modern complex living, we more and more are asked to keep a balance between the given, which although dynamic and changing represents the stable and the permanent, and the encounter with the unknown—the future descending on us. To adhere to faithful memory no longer serves as the healthy backbone of a steady person. On the contrary, we are asked to look at history and our own development as fumbling attempts to cope with what comes and as a series of miraculous constant readjustments that allow us to survive in the ocean of ignorance which is our condition.

Whatever explanations we may give to justify our creation of permanence, they cannot reduce to nothing the truth that we are faced all the time by what is not known and that we cannot adjust to it through the known. An organ as complex as our brain would not be needed if its purpose were to relate to the given, to the predictable, as if our way of learning was similar to a reflex response.

Still for centuries, if not millennia, a longing for a stable state of affairs has characterized the accumulated wisdom of most groups in spite of the defeat of this goal again and again. Because the mind and not the brain first gets involved in questions, the choice of easy challenges is possible. But the truth of life, which is connected to the truths of the brain, checks the choices by forcing the mind to meet the limitations of the proposal.

This is done as soon as the perceived and the conceived come into contact with each other, the perceived having a basis in the brain which is affected by outside energy and the conceived having the texture of images produced within the brain—and available to the self as energy. The self can always give strength to the perceived, but it can also ignore it and dwell totally in the conceived and deny the facts. When the perceived dominates, truth is asserted. When the conceived coincides with the perceived, peace is experienced, and truth is again asserted. When the conceived is at variance with the perceived and dominates, the self is deluded by the mind and may be led to assert untruths.

The mind can hold untruths while the brain says nothing. Retention of the conceived is as easy as retention of the perceived. (Perhaps it is harder to remember untruths than truths because with untruths there is not as good an agreement between the perceived and the conceived as when the given is integrated into the self.) Lies are obvious constructs, and to the mind they have the reality already found in all constructs. It is the practice of holding constructs that makes one remember lies and treat them like other stored mental material. That lies are not supported by reality makes them more vulnerable to the withdrawal of the energy loaned to them, and so they generate confusion more easily in the mind that invented them.

## The Place of Recognition

The retaining self on the whole works without effort. Retention can be considered a "natural" function of the self. If, in the case of language, the self <u>feels</u> the retentive effort in the act of deliberately paying ogdens, it is due to the fact that language has the built-in property that once an expression is found and uttered (or written) it does not have to be remembered. To counter this tendency of the mind—which lets the energy used by the brain return to the self once the expression is formed—it is necessary to give new amounts of energy to the material that is uttered or written. The self may then notice this extra dynamic (all the more so because languages contain means of producing equivalent expressions for almost all their utterances, so that any utterance is felt as less essential than if there were only one form) and experience the payment of ogdens as a distinct mental functioning.

Retention works better through acts of recognition (a power we examine in more detail in Chapter 8, "The Symbolizing Self") than through acts of remembering. And recognition is compatible with change and takes care of transformations, themselves compatible with both perception and expression. Therefore, in a world in flux, the self prefers recognition to perfect recall. Therefore, the self develops the device of paying ogdens to make remembering possible, and it goes on using recognition to meet the need of coping with changes that result from causes and events over which it has no control.

Since the perception of objects lit from changing sources, such as the sun, produces not one impact but any number of impacts, the truth of a situation requires the self to accept an array of impacts from the start and to alert itself to stressing some impacts and ignoring others, giving recognition a place in the act of knowing from the start. The retained impact is a compound, accepted without special fuss because it actually displays, to the self given to reality and truth, what is. From birth onwards, recognition and retention work together to make it possible for the individual to live in a world he knows is not made in the same way that the self made its soma, by continuous and conscious objectification. Recognition makes it possible to face that which changes all the time, that which goes to form classes of impressions in time, classes that differ from each other but are jointly christened as one, to be retained separately and together in harmony and compatibility.

This process of recognition is basic through all life and is needed to make many early learnings possible—such as acquiring the mother tongue, for instance.

This is why we can say that no one <u>remembers</u> his native tongue even though thousands of ogdens must have been paid to mobilize the nerve cells of the brain to store the words one cannot invent or, at least, does not invent.

## Aspects of Retention

Learning has clearly helped us here to study retention as a wider concept than simply memorizing, and it has given memory distinctive meanings that will reduce confusion when laboratories that study the brain work on it. In order to increase man's efficiency, researchers perhaps should not pursue the finding of chemicals that strengthen memory and concentrate instead on using the functionings of recognition and retention that have been cultivated by the self from the beginning, a process that is so well illustrated by one of the most common and most amazing learnings, that of the mother tongue.

The retention of words differs from the retention of other impacts because only a small amount of energy is mobilized for the former as compared with the amounts that accompany emotions and images of scenes. The retention of words also differs from other retentions because words are integrated differently. To reach words we have to ignore the components of the voice that normally not only accompany speech but also carry the largest amount of energy and are akin to emotions. Words require, therefore, an act of abstraction to isolate them so that they can affect the mind as entities. To be retained they need to be cleansed of what normally goes with them.

Emotions on the contrary, because they represent a here-and-now coagulation of energy, are separated from the whole self only by this act of coagulation. The images of a scene, likewise, do not require analysis and result from an indefinite number of simultaneous impacts that impinge upon the mind via the brain, an integrated and integrating instrument of the self.

This is why feelings do not seem to be retained in our memory. Instead, the remnants of the events that accompany feelings are more easily retained, and they may serve as triggers of an equivalent (actual or virtual) feeling—showing an economy of retention that gives back to the self any excess of energy to be used freely in future living.

In so-called pathological cases, this "unlocking" mechanism and the corresponding economies do not obtain any more. Obsession results from a dysfunction that for too long keeps too much energy attached to a perception, an evocation, a retained image, or flow of images associated with an event. The unlocking mechanism is, in this instance, defective. The self then seems compelled to handle a ruinous amount of energy without being able to find an approach that separates funding the receptacle with energy from funding the form of the receptacle. Absorbed as the self is in supplying itself to the abscess, no freedom is experienced, and the self that knows that health and freedom go together now knows a dynamics of the self contrary to normal living. Thus, it considers itself to be sick. The more so in that the self is simultaneously witnessing many normal Acts of living which are not affected by the obsession. The release of the locking mechanism, which has closed the movement of energy upon itself, may require only a very small intervention, provided it is done at the right place at the right time. A needle at one of the Chinese points or at one of the brain locations endowed with the survey and supervision of energy shifts within the self, may suffice in certain cases.

All of us know some kind of abscess of the mind which is requiring too much energy, and we know that retention is being used to keep alive what should have been let go into our memory to join the integrated self at work. The realm of the mind in which this occurs is simultaneously affectivity and intellectuality. Because it is affectivity, it asks us to pay attention to the amounts of energy involved, and because it is intellectuality, it tells us to feel hopeless in the face of a dysfunction that demands that we do deliberately what until now seemed to come from a know-how that automatically took care of itself.

The awareness of the self keeping alive a part of one's past by pouring energy into networks that can hold only tenuous amounts of energy brings to the fore the process of revivifying any set of existing functionings or activating the memory for special uses. The retained forms do not in fact return the same content to the self because the amount of energy that surfaces is related to the energy poured into the forms, and memory normally returns different contents simply because each return is accompanied by the awareness of "now," which differs on every occasion of recall. Fidelity is therefore almost incompatible with recalls, which successively transform the retained. The special training that individuals spontaneously give themselves may provide them with a faithful memory, but this ultimately may not be better for the job of living in a changing world than is a memory that reconstructs (around enough retained material) one or other of the important aspects of the events connected with the retention, this reconstruction then serving as a trigger.

In our complex life, total retention and faithful recall may sometimes be what is required; at other times, our intelligence of the moment selects from the retained what is proper for the circumstances. Far from being a taped succession of what happened in time in our life, memory and recall are functions serving the demands of the moment. Selective forgetfulness is one of the functions of the mind. The mind can manage to forget one item linked to many others, to separate, as it does in the case of songs, what was never separated to begin with and recall either the words or the tune or a mixture of separate elements. The self knows what is stored, but it does not always know just how to bring back what is resisting recall.

Triggering is a property of the self in relation to memory. The retained elements can be triggered into consciousness by all sorts of devices so that the content of a recall, which of course first depends on the overall materials retained, can bring together in the consciousness much that was not previsible. Associations, "free" associations, serve to prove the existence of the triggering device as well as the variability of the content that comes back to consciousness.

The mystery of memory and its diverse functionings remains almost as great after all this study as at the start, but something is certainly clearer: that only by recognizing the complexity of the workings of the mind and the complex dynamics within it, on top of the intricacies of the brain, shall we be in a position to penetrate the universe of memory a little.

The simplistic view that we simply tape-record our life is misleading and singularly unhelpful.

# 7 The Intelligent Self

Rather than reach intelligence through its performance, which includes many other functionings, we shall look at the self and some of its activities as they become explicit and find in them what can be singularly qualified as intelligence. For intelligence is not a scholastic attribute, even if it was first quantified in tests for schools.

## What Intelligence Does

The self can become aware very early that in a given situation one can do this or that to learn how what to do to improve a functioning (to one's own satisfaction). We shall place the functioning of intelligence in this dialogue with oneself about what one is doing, the aim of which is to bring about a change that will better integrate one's actions in a situation.

For example, a woman who has just had her first baby and wants to give it the first meal at her breast may provide the baby with an opportunity to note that the pumping he is now learning to perform will be easier if he acts on his mouth or lower jaw in such-and-such a manner. To take the opportunity to move from purely mechanical behavior to modified behavior more in keeping with the demands and possibilities of the situation is to be intelligent.

Intelligence may have shown itself earlier, say, when the self <u>in utero</u> noted the umbilical cord and managed to move in the space without becoming entangled, but we shall be concerned here only with postnatal learnings—that is, during most of our sometimes long lives.

Acquainted with the self and its dynamic, and reaching the dynamics in what has been objectified, intelligence becomes one of the ways of knowing Reality. But only while it is doing its job. Both the self and intelligence can mobilize the stored self, the potential, to cope with a perceived challenge. But intelligence is the here-and-now agent of the self, knowingly and deliberately doing a job on those parts of the self that are directly involved in a situation, and it is not concerned with anything else simultaneously at work in the self, which remains in the domain of the self.

Intelligence of the self at work produces the shaded ways of study that permit intelligence to know itself as it is and to justify its name. Although the connections between the self, awareness, intelligence, and many other attributes must be taken into account in producing a true model of actual human living, they may lead to the recognition that through the self knowing itself each of the attributes may also know itself.

The self has awareness; awareness has it too; intelligence has it too. The self is intelligent; so intelligence can know itself by the self becoming aware of its reality within itself.

The task for us today is to see ourselves attempting to grasp what the self does for each of us, and to make explicit our intelligence of the self in its totality engaged in the total act of living a human life.

## The Reach of Intelligence

The self has intelligence because the self is much more than all its objectifications and the activities in them and among them. It has awareness, and when it engages in an activity, it can at once note that energy is available within itself, and if appropriate it can send some of the energy to involve functionings not yet involved in the activity. It is the functioning of intelligence to come in when it is not necessarily engaged and to add its "intelligence" or understanding of how to cope best with what the self is involved in.

The past is present in the use of all that is in the soma, the brain, the mind; the present activity is sustained by concentration, by selection of what to use, and by using it; the future is represented by intelligence that surveys the manner in which the present uses the past and, if need be, brings more of the past to bear in the situation or affects the concentration in the activity and the selection of what to use in it.

## II
### The Brain Alone Cannot Generate a Complex Human Life

Intelligence is not an object. No more than is awareness or concentration. But it is an attribute of the self that only the self can sense and recognize in the multiple appearances of its manifestations. The self, giving itself the task of noticing how it is engaged in what it is doing and of reporting to the part of the self outside the concentration, acknowledges the functioning of intelligence as distinct from all other functionings and starts undertaking its study at various moments in its life.

The self knows its intelligence long before it calls it that. It soon discovers it as one of its functionings, but a functioning that is two stages removed from the somatic structures of the self. The field of intelligence is not directly what the organs do with themselves, a job that has been delegated to the functions of the brain; rather, its field is the supervision of situations so as to call in functions other than those the brain has called in, or to agree with the brain in its organization of the activity. Because errors exist, the self has given itself functionings that detect them and put them right. Because dependence exists and much that impinges upon us is outside our control, causes for errors are plentiful. Because the self transcends all its involvements and has surplus energy, it can reduce the chances of error and, instead of correcting errors after they occur, call in a surveyor who watches the way the self's potential is put at the service of its involvements. Intelligence does this, not the brain.

The self that has the power to objectify may give intelligence somatic support, by adding new layers to the brain, or by increasing the flexibility of existing links, or by introducing links where none existed. Intelligence may dwell in the yet uncommitted cells that are already endowed with all the circuitry that can make them into a superior integrator, an agent having access to more of the objectified self than the previous integrations. When this happens, the soma, memory, and other components of the self will obey the intelligence.

But since at various moments of our evolution we have always had more brain than has been committed to functionings, the self has intermingled intelligence with all other experiences of itself.

There is intelligent eating and intelligent control of the digestive tube so that the self disciplines itself to produce socially acceptable forms of feeding and evacuating. There is room for intelligent breathing to avoid being out of breath in situations not calling for it or to cope with new demands on the old functioning. There is room for intelligent seeing, hearing, feeling, and so on.

The main learning is that intelligence is associated with all of living and that it can come in if it is let in.

## Misuses of Intelligence

Other functionings of the self may prevent the functioning of intelligence, particularly adherence to the past. We can make ourselves stupid, that is, as if we had no intelligence, by clinging to behaviors or concepts that do not demand such adherence. But intelligence can also intervene to mobilize the will to take us out of our adherence.

Self-interest—which in a person who is true to life is a definite guide—can become different from the self's best interest, and it can lead so-called intelligent people to stupid acts or actions. So we may distinguish intelligent intelligence and stupid intelligence. For example, making A's at school in activities irrelevant to the broad demands of life demonstrates stupid intelligence, while dropping out at school may be proof of intelligent intelligence. How many people who are known to be gifted and endowed have failed to bend towards their best interest by not letting their intelligence look into the moves needed to meet what they saw as their self-interest. So many scientists are among those who prefer the pursuit of their ambitions to the pursuit of truth. So many business people, too, believe that climbing the corporate scale is proof of being in the market and do not look at the reality of the market.

Intelligence is present from the beginning of a change until it is implemented. The capacity to make transformations, which proves the presence of intelligence, also enables one to reach an understanding of situations, because the only successful transformations are those that belong to the situations and their dynamics. A person subject to fits of anger at home may show calm and not be irritated in places where his perceptions suggest that control is to be preferred.

At school a given subtraction may suggest a transformation to a pupil that will make the problem immediately answerable and with certainty that the answer is correct. But unless there is understanding, no one attempts transformations. As long as one has no access to what is behind the appearances, the only approaches are inaction and fear or maintenance of the given.

Most students who show a lack of understanding in compulsory subjects at school have mistaken this lack of understanding for a lack of intelligence in them-selves. Intelligence is often synonymous with understanding. The reason for the close connection between a word describing a function of the self in many activities (intelligence) and a word describing a specific state in the self's involvement (understanding), comes from the fact that the presence of intelligence felt in that state of involvement generates a conviction of understanding and its sequel of peace, excitement, and the mobilization of energy to move ahead.

Intelligence is needed to drop a trial effort because of an error and to produce another opportunity for a different trial. In a crude trial-and-error method, guidance comes as much from intelligence as it does in the virtual (mental) disentanglement that precedes a one-shot successful attempt. Trial and error would lead nowhere were it not for the working of intelligence which records the attempts and the results to avoid a mere repetition of unsuccessful trials.

Trial and error is an intelligent way of meeting the unknown.

Drill and repetition, on the contrary, deny its existence.

That is why drill and repetition lead to fatal encounters with skills at school and why years spent in classrooms have almost nothing to show for them. Intelligence is a functioning of the self and thus everybody's birthright, and to deny intelligence where learning takes place is to sterilize the process.

Intelligence as a quality of the self can be allowed to do its proper work or be prevented by actions from within or without—mostly from within, when the self allows distractions to occupy it.

Intelligence can be encouraged to function again as soon as it is recognized as a property of the self and not, as has been maintained again and again, a socio-economic factor or a racial factor. Intelligence does not grow; it either functions well or it does not. Whenever a behavior is seen as it is, it functions well. Whenever the self gets involved in what is not reality, it does not function, and the unhappy consequences follow from this misuse of what the self has and owns.

Babies are extremely intelligent and do the right things in many involvements since they know their place in the world—they know what is theirs and what is out of their control. They spontaneously suspend judgment in contact with the unknown, a proper functioning of intelligence. They listen carefully and guess cautiously, noticing clues that tell them they should pursue or drop an idea—other functionings of intelligence. They know that they have to be involved by looking, listening, exploring, before they can discriminate impacts—yet another functioning of intelligence.

They do not feel mistakes are out of place in learning; on the contrary, they recognize mistakes as indicators that more work needs to be done in the area they are involved in. Nor do they make the errors that misguided people make: they do not treat the unknown as if it were known, other people as if they did not exist (or will respond to one's desires only in order to satisfy them), life as if it were already structured by the little one has achieved.

## Awareness at the Gate

The work of intelligence is as varied as man's perceptions of the world and the numerous functionings available to him. In every involvement it contributes to check the automatization that uniformizes and eliminates the singular. Thus, it is at the source of the questions "why?" and "how?" When the self is involved in some happening, these two questions keep the self on the job and nourish the continuation of human living. ("What?" differs from "how?" only in so far as it seeks a localization among a defined set of possibilities.)

Intelligence not only chooses from what is available, it also makes available what is compatible with the given and will serve the purpose of the involvement. Hence, intelligence creates forms for the self that are more subtle than the links in the brain between the content of the cells, but it is capable also of mobilizing these links by giving them the forms it has created.

This capacity makes explicit the two-stage remoteness of intelligence from the somatic structures: the brain oversees the structures, intelligence surveys the brain's activity and can go beyond it. It also gives the world of intelligence a reality accessible to the self, the so-called individual "intellect" that we shall study later (in Chapter 9). Intelligence as a presence of the self in the brain knows itself as distinct from the functionings of the brain, however subtle its links with the latest neurons that were produced. It can know itself and discover that it can essentially transcend the given and can call in enough energy to produce a project or, by totally absorbing the committed energy back into the self, reduce it to nothing, with no track left in the self.

Not only must the amounts of energy be minute in order not to be assimilated to the linkages in the brain, but the forms that intelligence temporarily gives to them are the result of this mental separation of energy from the lot of energy available for mental consideration. In the molecular realm, it is the kind of process that makes surface tension capable of separating drops of water one from another, the tension disappearing when the drops merge into a larger amount.

Intelligence, by being two stages removed from the self's somatic objectification, provides the self with new possibilities at all levels, and it therefore can transform the individual by making him do more than was inscribed in him by heredity. Intelligence works out human mutations that cost very little in energy. But instead of producing new species compatible with the environment, it produces a new person capable of seeing new opportunities in the environment it can create. For intelligence has reached the dynamics of the world and acts upon the dynamics instead of on the world and obtains its results because of this, making truth more visible at the same time.

If there is a somatic intelligence, there is also an intelligence of actions, an intelligence of feelings, of thoughts, of relationships, of organization, of decision making, of compromise, of how much to delegate and how much to objectify, of how to treat the learning of skills and the learning about others; there is an intelligence of meeting different challenges differently, of making the self one at the same time that it is adaptable, and so on. Intelligence manifests itself in life precisely by discovering that it is not a thing on its own but an attribute of the self illuminating or illumining each "moment" of involvement of the self in the life of the person from conception.

To know intelligence through memory of performance is not an intelligent movement of the self. Rather, it misses the point and accumulates errors because of a basic mistake. The role of intelligence is to remain a quality and thus to escape quantification. Intelligence cannot be accumulated. It can only renew itself in the contact of true life challenges. Once it is held to be identical to itself—is what it has achieved—then it has been given an alien form, made what it is not, and therefore sterilized.

Presented with this paradox, that intelligence can be stupid, we can understand how it is that when the self allows itself to be distracted, to use its time to accumulate objectifications indiscriminately or to do only what is imposed by circumstances and other people, intelligence stops to function as the aspect of the self that knows what needs to be done—that is, more simply, stops to function.

## II
### The Brain Alone Cannot Generate a Complex Human Life

The self can know intelligence at work and recognize that problem-solving, for example, is one of the jobs of intelligence—but only one job, and certainly not a constant one, unless the word problem covers all kinds of perceived challenges. To say "intelligence is for problem solving" is tautological. But even if we shift from a quality of the self to its activities, we must note that the only "problems" that have been suggested to "measure" intelligence are either scholastic or professional; they exclude somatic, affective, social intelligence problems, all of which challenge us more often than do other problems and much earlier and persistently than others.

Intelligence partakes of awareness but differs from it in that intelligence has an active role beyond the knowing role. Only when it directs the will into action, mental action (even if this is to refrain from certain actions), can intelligence be said to be present. Since the self owns awareness and initiative, intelligence can be seen as awareness and initiative made into one awareness that is always present, with initiative brought in by linking what one is engaged in with what one finds in the potential of the self, whether a perception of the world or of oneself. It would perhaps help everyone to consider intelligence as a functioning of awareness so that this essential component is maintained, but nothing would be gained in understanding if the component of initiative were to be left out. Man has known this for a long time, and he took the initiative of suggesting a new label for the particular awareness that is involved in what the self perceives in order to declare that the self is doing its job or to call in what might put it right.

Intelligence is awareness at the gate watching the flow of life, allowing passage to what works and taking what is in need of repair to the workshop.

Intelligence is needed because of the self/world duality. Paradoxically, its function produces the possibility of a monistic view of the universe where the self understands its own role in making out of its perceptions a world that very closely resembles the assumed world outside.

Intelligence is needed to maintain the balance of the outside world within and the outside world without. Only intelligence can cope with both since intelligence alone is two stages removed from the self's objectifications, looking at them as the way the self perceives the outside world and looking at the functionings as the presence of the self in the objectifications, letting them do what it wishes.

# 8 The Symbolizing Self

Very early in human life it is possible to observe a cooperation between the free self and some of the freer functionings of the brain, which are also actions of the self. At this stage there are new learning opportunities that mark the growth of the self, making it capable of attempting broader tasks, more complex ones more competently.

## The Power of Recognition

As we see in experiments in gestalt psychology, it is possible for an animal to be deluded, to make faulty judgments, and to pay for the consequences of its beliefs. But man systematizes his search of how much of a perception is sufficient to trigger the whole.

This way of knowing is called "recognition" (which we briefly encountered in Chapter 6), and its development, which takes place as soon as perception is functional, serves all future growth of the mind. The word re-cognition, although formed from "cognition" and the repeat prefix "re," has a broader meaning than "knowing again." Its main meaning is that something is known even though elements that might prevent knowing have been encountered. Recognition is a power of the self that needs opportunities to exercise itself, and while it is becoming an instrument of the self to be applied to all aspects of life, it works on the proper functionings of the brain to give them the endowments needed for the tasks ahead.

Since the self knows how to use the nervous system to send signals to the periphery and to regulate the amount of energy dispatched, it can activate some sensory areas selectively and, during sleep, study how much of the system needs activating for a cluster of neurons to become excited. Much of the "meaningless" oneiric activity that takes place every time we sleep can be counted as part of this study. As soon as we assume that this activity may have a function, we offer ourselves an opportunity to meet more of the self and its workings.

Most of our dreams are not recalled, and consciousness in the waking state has no access to them. If we attempt to find their significance for the self (their functioning being understood as an inner activation of the sense organs, the reverse of what happens in the waking state), we see that it is perfectly possible for the self to use the opportunity of being withdrawn from the world of sensation to study the energizing of the sense organs with the basic energy from the neurons. Through the triggering that follows, the self recognizes images that resemble the direct impacts that originated in the world.

There is no need for anyone besides oneself in this kind of energy dialogue between the self and the sense organs. It is part of the expertise of the self because of the intimacy of the self with its soma and functionings. It is also part of the economics of energy practiced from conception, to get as much as possible for as small an expenditure as possible.

Clearly, dreams can as easily be viewed as being related to the aggression of the outside on the self as they can be conceived as the expression of the self withdrawn into its own system, at work on its dynamics. Because babies, a few months after birth, play games of make-believe in which they involve their parents rather than the other way round, we have a factual basis for knowing that the self is educating itself during these months in the dosage of energy that is needed to replace the full amount of the energy of impacts in order to generate awareness of the corresponding reality.

This evocation of images, which fills the brain with substitutes for the world, precedes the act of re-cognition and coordinates with it. In terms of the expenditure of energy, it improves the functioning of those parts of the brain that are involved and thus makes more of the brain excitable for an equal expenditure of energy. This education results from the learning done at night, in sleep, when the self has no one to please and its only job is to educate itself to the best of its ability. The benefit for the waking state is that recognition is available, giving more capacity to achieve more with less.

In the process of generating recognition, the self can become aware that in the waking state as well as in sleep there is no need to be given everything of anything to be able to evoke the whole. The self engages in dialogues with the impacts from outside and recognizes that it can discover new ways of using itself alongside a waking-state awareness of what is being done.

In particular, the self acknowledges that impressions from classes as well as temporal sequences (for example, the light in a room, which changes for no reason as far as the baby is concerned) generates different impressions, but that they all may belong to each other through certain links. And soon it is possible to link impressions received <u>via</u> different sense organs and use one to evoke another, or even a whole class of impressions in one go.

## The Human Creation of Symbolism

Soon this becomes a way of knowing held dear by the self since it explodes boundaries and indicates a new power accompanied with the well-known experience of freedom. The world is suddenly crisscrossed with sound impressions that evoke visual images and vice-versa, smells that trigger scenes containing many components that may involve all the sense and vice-versa, and so on. From now on the self, aware of such dynamics, will use it in all the circumstances that are compatible with it. The time when such an awareness will be considered finally available depends on a number of factors, including the opportunities for entertaining the formation of multidimensional images. Sleep makes its contribution, but exercises in the waking state will help too.

For instance, the baby takes advantage of being tossed around in the arms of adults to collect impressions of the world that are not "normal" in his hours on his back. He retains smells and associates them with both the different kinds of pressures on his skin created by the hands that handle him and the visual images, or sounds, or both, that are linked to these impressions. He cannot fail to know that the many centers that are simultaneously excited in his brain form a complex that may be triggered by any one of the components in the complex.

This awareness, and the exercise of measuring energy during sleep, blend together to form the foundation of a new power that the self will acknowledge and that outsiders will call <u>symbolization.</u>

In its basic functioning, symbolism is the reduction in the number of components that are needed to trigger spontaneously masses of the stored-up elements that are substitutes for reality. Because of other functionings these masses do not always have to be one and the same set. But the meaning of symbolism or symbolization is not touched by the actual content of the evocation. The self has taken itself another step away from the initial functioning of the brain with which it was dialoguing and has discovered that if the triggering is kept latent, the element that triggers can act as a symbol for various available responses. Practice with the symbols generates a new universe that did not exist in the brain or in the self, a truly human creation that involves a more educated self and brain because they now can do what they could not do previously.

The reality of symbols is acknowledged in the way of all other realities: directly by the self which has done all the work, and by the successive involvements that take the self to the energy of the cosmos found in the molecules of the cells of the soma.

Once these involvements are integrated, as they are through the process of learning, it is to be expected that if the physico-chemical basis is affected by some outside intervention, it can trigger masses of images which in turn trigger symbols and the unique self that formed them, thus attributing to the aggression properties that belong to the objectified self and conversely. We may believe that we come to know the brain through such interventions.

## The Power of Symbolism

Because the self finds symbols more convenient to handle than the associated masses which are the stuff of life, a radical transformation follows a decision to dedicate oneself to the life of the symbols rather than to the experiencing of their actual content-classes.

Humanity can be subdivided into classes according to the way that individuals choose to relate to symbols. From time immemorial this has been an effective way of creating cleavages between men and women. Priests, for example, are dedicated to the manipulation of symbols and their expressions. A hierarchy of power results from the differing skills in handling symbols, starting at the top with those who can do most with the least down to those who cannot save much energy by reference to the virtual or who have not yet noticed that such reality exists. A birthright is denied to some people because it is not brought to consciousness at the moment of possible awareness.

When we examine the modern concept of "conditioned reflex," we see at once the mechanism of symbolization at work, but it remains an isolated awareness that cannot illumine a self distracted by the separation of the awareness from the self (itself not recognized as a reality). A "symbol" can trigger, and therefore condition unrelated biological functionings, but since it is not a symbol in the sense developed here, the reality of the phenomenon is mistaken, and all efforts to understand the activity of learning in Pavlovian terms can lead nowhere. Learning is not the result of conditioning. Symbols are not arbitrary signs. Only awareness can open the gates of the mind, and symbols, by construction, can let the flow of mental stuff come in. Learning to concentrate on the symbols and to place brakes on the gates so that they open only at will is the truth about man and the opposite of conditioning. Nevertheless, conditioning can take place in man because the self has provided a procedure that can affect some link in the nervous system.

As soon as the self has recognized how to use its energy through symbols, it can repeat the process at the level of symbols and reduce even further the cost of triggering the underlying hierarchies. This can take place only if the self acknowledged the set of symbols that may be replaced by a new symbol and recognizes that the one symbol is endowed with a dynamics that makes it a substitute for the set. Then it learns again to activate the brakes that render the supporting set of symbols potential while allowing the self to work on the symbol of symbols.

Perhaps this process can be repeated a number of times.

We shall see some examples when we study the intellectual self in Chapter 10.

## The Place of Symbolism

The role of symbolism in human life is cardinal. It could come about only because the self has the capacity to dwell simultaneously in a number of its objectified forms and in itself as free energy. Therefore, the self always has open to it the opportunity of meeting the new and entertaining it with what the self is so as to change, through integration, what it was into a new "is." This awareness has been cryptically expressed by saying that man is "becoming."

By recognizing the world of symbols as belonging to the self, we have stated that we cannot fail to find symbols intermingled with all the life of the mind and that through them we notice the dual movement of integrating the past while freeing the self towards wider destinies.

We find symbols at work in all intellectual activities, in the creation of languages as well as in their learning, in mathematical activity, in the elaboration of the sciences, in the awareness of music, of art, of religion, in the making of all sorts of models, including those of man. We shall find symbols alongside thought and alongside action in all those human activities that have created history and opened up the future to a different and a new living that is much more aware of itself and of what it can do through its education of awareness.

Because so much more needs to be said about the symbolizing self, we shall spread our study of it over a number of subsequent chapters devoted primarily to more special considerations. The shortness of this exposition should not be taken to signify the relative unimportance of symbols and symbolization. They constitute a cardinal turning point in man's evolution, when he became aware of the functioning that made it possible for him to grasps the existence of symbols.

# 9 The Intellectual Self

In ancient Greece it was Aristotle who knew most about the functioning of the intellect. In western Europe it was Descartes. Many philosophers in all civilizations have written a great deal about the intellect. There may still be room for one more view of it.

In this book we look at human living in all planes and all realms by the light of the self and awareness and all the functionings connected to the objectified self. The brain is an instrument that can do many things and can do them very well. But because the self transcends its own structure and its own functionings, when we use the self as the generator of human living, we go beyond the brain, and perhaps even affect the brain by adding to it other structures or functionings. We can say that man's life, his living, makes more brain so that it will serve him more adequately in the new state of awareness he has reached.

Hence, from our viewpoint, rather than seeing human life as a by-product of biological evolution, we see structural biological evolution as the necessary accompaniment of the self that knows itself and finds itself aware of a functioning for which it gives itself a biological support. Truly, the "function creates the organ."

But the brain has only the possibilities it has while the self seems capable of transcending itself even as it remains in contact with the soma and uses all it has got from it. In some of its acts of transcendence, the self has created, out of itself, awarenesses that could be given reality in the self by simply linking the new with the old.

Symbols gain their reality this way.

Symbols of symbols are the stuff of a new functioning of the self. The part of the self that entertains them we shall call the <u>intellect</u>, and the corresponding aspect of life, the intellectual life of the self.

## The Intellect at Work: Learning the Mother Tongue

Once more the reality of all this is in the self, and its translation into perceptible reality results from the self's contact with its objectifications. Other men of my age, in my environment, at this time in history, may see all this reality very differently from people of a different age, place, and time. A baby who is not yet aware of his sociocultural milieu may see the reality of symbols of symbols as I do, simply through the closeness of the contact between his self and reality. This closeness can be lost in acts of concrete living in a particular milieu and needs to be conquered again.

Perhaps the key to understanding how babies manage to learn their mother's tongue is their immediate recognition of the dynamics of symbols of symbols (when they do not interfere with it as adults do). Intellectual living is as much the realm of babies as of adult scientists and philosophers.

Let us consider again the extraordinary achievement of learning the mother tongue.

What is required of anyone attempting to fathom the verbal universe is the recognition that there are two universes of perception that he has to associate in such a way that some elements of one correspond in some precise manner to some elements of the other.

First let us look at the universes themselves. One is made of all the perceptions belonging to the self-in-the-world. These include the perceptions that reach the self through the sense organs as well as those originating within the self and known for what they are. The meaning of each of the latter perceptions is immediate and direct, does not require interpretation, and is known by some energy attribute of which the brain has been apprised. The external impacts also gain their meaning through energy, the energy they bring with them. They educate the brain to know them as color, shape, relief, consistency, sound duration, intensity, and so on, all describable in terms of energy.

This first universe can be defined as the universe of direct perceptions, and it provides what we shall call the first class of perceptible meanings. It is the universe to which the deaf and the blind have access in spite of their so-called handicaps.

The second universe is also a universe of perceptions, but it is not possible to know this universe through its energy content, for its energy has not been a consideration in its inception. These perceptions exist because other selves put their utterances into circulation and the utterances reach the ears of hearers. Until a hearer re-cognizes that he has to shake the impact on his ears free of all its attributes except the one that he can carry with his voice and utter, he will not know what reality he is contemplating.

To make himself ready for this task, the baby has spontaneously discovered that he can coordinate his system of utterances with a system of heard sounds, made by himself but recognized as coming from outside. For a few months he has studied how his self—which knows his utterances as vocal and controlled by voluntary changes at the level of the larynx, the mouth, and the lungs—can recognize his utterances auditorally. Until he recognizes with his ear what he utters, and he re-cognizes what he hears in terms of his own voice production, he does not have the double system of utterances/sounds in which each can trigger the other and each can play the role of symbol for the other. Energy contents can be matched in this system, and knowledge is direct.

Once the baby lets himself be moved by what other people utter, he can use his functioning to stress and ignore so as to recognize something he knows in what strikes his ears. When this is filtered from the rest and retained, it becomes part of the universe that comes from outside but is perceptible as it is, that is, arbitrary sounds that are recognizable by their features but that cannot trigger any meaning beyond the fact of resemblance.

All this the baby, plunged in his environment, can do by himself.

To enter the language of his environment, he must create a new functioning, and this conscious operation will take several months, becoming easier every day.

Alerted to the need to listen and to hear—to ignore pitch, timber, stress, melody, intonation, and to stress the sound carried by the voices—he also has to note all the concomitants of the utterance—the atmosphere, the content of the space around, the sequence of sounds, the referential present—and guess that the sounds he hears are connected with some action, some object, some movement, and produced only because of this concomitant. Fortunately, these tasks are akin to those the baby does spontaneously by himself.

He knows concentration and how to apply it to reduce the field that impinges on him. He knows how to hold one sound and let all the others slip through his mind. He can recognize that some property of the voice can be found in previous impacts on his ear. He can analyze a sound and find the elements in it that he already knows how to utter. He recognizes if some attribute of his field of perception seems to be present when a particular sound is uttered by others, and he can stress the concomitance, making it an instrument in his study. He can put together several of these know-hows and come up with an utterance of his own, summing-up his synthesis. He then scrutinizes the faces of others or their responses to know whether his guess was right. If it was, he integrates the three elements (synthesis, utterance, and response) and has a label for a perceived meaning. He has changed himself by knowing that he can now evoke the meaning; he can use it to trigger the sound he has produced and conversely can trigger the meaning by evoking or uttering the sound.

Although the sound is arbitrary, its reality is not. Nor is the evocation of the perceptions. Nor is the link between the evocation and the sound. The new unit, similar to so many other functionings of the self, gives the self an opportunity to use the brain for what it can do. The word will be assigned to memory by the payment of an ogden. A link will relate this retained word to a retained image (or feeling or class of impressions) through the well-practiced functioning of the brain that makes the one a trigger for the other.

As more and more of these operations of the self generate dual networks in the brain (one network of sounds, one network of evocations), the baby learns how to play the game of acting on one to trigger the other. He learns to speak what he feels or perceives or acts or wills. He learns to understand through these same realities what other people are conveying through their words.

Naturally a great deal more is involved in this learning. (Again I can refer readers to earlier publications of mine, <u>The Universe of Babies</u> in particular.) What I want to illustrate here is that although words are not symbols of anything, the self treats them as if they had a reality that, like symbols, were two stages removed from perception.

On the one hand, the sounds of words must be held for no other reason than their consistency, and they are acknowledged to have only the reality of being retainable (through a special property of the brain). On the other hand, unnecessary (that is, invented) connections are established and maintained between some content of the mind, some stored-up material in the brain, and these arbitrary signs. A system of such signs and the corresponding complex system of mobilized mental content are linked together into a dual system of mutual triggers. This can be worked on so that the self can establish brakes on the evocation and free itself to concentrate on the flow of words as such. The act of speaking is then separated from the constructed dual system and becomes an attribute of the self from then on. So much so that words are treated as symbols when they are only signs—arbitrary signs at that. But they are easily mistaken for symbols because of their similarity to the functioning of symbols.

Language is the best possible example of an intellectual activity of the self. The arbitrariness of vocabulary requires that we work on a plane removed from the supply of experience and meaning that we have gathered in the making of the soma. In all other mental activities, symbols are directly connected with this supply and can trigger something of it. Since babies learn to speak—sometimes at the age of one or two—the functionings required to transform a system of pairs of percepts into a dynamic and highly organized voluntary system (where perceived meanings become triggers of flows of sounds) must be considered as resulting solely from the awareness of the self at work in its other manifestations.

We have to acknowledge that by learning to speak, a baby demonstrates that the intellectual self is not produced by schools and scholastic work, in contact with learned elders, but is at work as soon as these functionings, twice removed from the soma, can surge into the self to be noticed by it.

Of course, as in all other learnings, to have achieved speech frees the self to use it to conquer other fields of manifestation. Learning how to relate to one's language may go on for the rest of one's life, but the intellectual feat that constructed the elaborate system of words, stresses, phrasings, melody, structures, equivalent expressions; the algebra of attributes regulating the uses of adjectives, the algebra of classes applying to nouns, the algebra of substitutions operating on pronouns, the awareness of time for tenses, or space and time-relations for prepositions, the shaded sequences of phrases associated with conjunctions, the judgment of the nuances produced when adjectives qualify nouns and adverbs qualify verbs—this intellectual feat must lead us to the conclusion that the intellect is an early product of the self working on itself.

## The Intellect and the Algebra of Language and Mathematics

Among the discoveries made when we study how babies learn to speak the language of the environment, the one that refers to algebra seems most closely related to seeing that an intellectual self is the birthright of all men. Long before algebra became a chapter of mathematics, it had been used by men everywhere. Indeed, the many thousands of languages spoken on Earth today, and probably all those lost in the past, display one property in common: from a very small number of distinct sounds, very many other sounds can be formed by mental operations that, when they are formalized, belong in a book of algebra under the heading, "combinations and permutations."

Because the self, once it uttered sounds, became aware that it could distinguish them by any of the main properties it could objectify, it mingled the many possible operations of "variations on the sounds," and at different places, it chose to perpetuate one or other of the resulting alternatives. Thus, there are languages in which sounds are distinguished by duration, others that are distinguished by the associated pitch or tone, others by repetition, others by nasalization, others by the combination of some or all of these.

But after selecting the particular basis to build on, all languages chose to produce utterances that were distinguished by the order of the composite sounds. Since it was clear that the order of sounds is perceptible, order gave an easy way of producing more than one word with the same choice of sounds (an example in English is the triplet <u>apt</u>, <u>pat</u>, tap; in Spanish <u>son</u> and <u>nos</u>, <u>una</u>, and <u>aun</u>; in Hindi <u>rama</u> and <u>mara</u>; in Mandarin <u>aw</u> and <u>wa</u>; and so on).

In English many words are made with one group of sounds (a word) preceded by various simple sounds: <u>pill</u>, <u>till</u>, <u>sill</u>, <u>mill</u>, <u>fill</u>, <u>dill</u>, <u>will</u>, <u>kill</u>, <u>rill</u>, <u>hill</u>, <u>gill</u>, <u>chill</u>, <u>quill</u> is one example; <u>old</u>, <u>told</u>, <u>sold</u>, <u>mold</u>, <u>fold</u>, <u>cold</u>, <u>hold</u>, <u>gold</u> is another. Other words are the sound reversal of each other, as for example <u>lick</u> and <u>kill</u>, <u>sick</u> and <u>kiss</u>. This facility with a creative instrument, which is found in all languages and which has been studied (much after its development) under the label of algebra, is also found in the awareness of very young children in their cribs. As soon as two sounds can be uttered, one after the other, the baby can notice the reality of their order and can recognize the two possible permutations as different, each of them retainable and available for use later when the individual meets the historic development of sounds as language.

Mathematicians have recently been engaged in the examination of the content of their historic objectifications, and they have found that most of these objectifications could be rebuilt from a small number of irreducible structures. Mathematicians conceive of algebra as the dynamic structure, the only one that can permit a departure from the static. Indeed, without it there could not be any mathematics. Nor could there be any languages. In fact, because mathematics and language (and many other manifestations of the self) are products of the mind, the use of algebra as an essential component of both suggests that algebra is an attribute of the self when it is involved in the systematic use of alterations—transformations—and in the construction of its objectifications beyond the somatic self (and no doubt even before).

The intellectual self dwells in the universe of the intellect, sitting beyond the brain in the temporal sequences of the self, having access not only to what the brain can offer but also to what can be done constructing intellectual layers where symbols, symbols of symbols, symbols of symbols of symbols, etc., are proposed for the self's attention.

Modern mathematics has been doing exactly the same thing in the realm of hierarchies of abstractions, moving from operations on numbers to operations on operations, from groups to groupoids then to categories, from integrals to totalization, trying all the while to find the most naked structure from which all others will be formed by the induction of another structure.

At the same time, epistemology has moved towards looking at the mind as the generator of all knowledge through the dynamics it adds to what it extracts from experience. Epistemology also sees algebra as present in all mental activities because algebra is another way of speaking of the dynamics that must be present if the self is energy. Experience involves the soma and the brain, and the dynamics of the self sheds light on both.

## The Intellect Makes the Sciences

Awareness of experience, from which symbols can be formed by reducing the content to a virtual (mental) presence and adding a dynamics compatible with the symbols, seems to have been the basis of all the sciences. "To know" in each science is to let the self examine experience, shake it free of as many individualizing attributes as possible, and apply to it the dynamics of transformation that is compatible with the content that remains.

Physics is a way of knowing what the brain has stored as sensory perceptions, but is removed far enough from the content to make it possible to study weight when heaviness is experienced, to study heat when warmth or coldness are experienced, to study acoustics when impacts on the ear are experienced, and so on. Physics is a function of the intellect precisely because it reduces the brain's contact with experience by replacing experience with a substitute. "Light" is equivalent to a symbol of all the actual photons that strike the retina. Working on the substitute makes it possible to have experiments in lieu of experience and to end up with a law instead of just a behavior.

The natural sciences began as the codification of the awarenesses that were present when the self experienced its connection with the environment—that is, when the content of the brain was transformed through experience. But the intellect soon found that one quality that the self could know could be connected to all the other qualities and could transform them into quantities. As a result, science was mistakenly said to study only the measurable, the quantifiable, even when no true measure existed (as in finding temperature). Still, physicists knew that they first had to be aware of quality and to become vulnerable to alterations in states, before they could assert the existence of a phenomenon and before they could look for the measurable variable (which, in many cases, they found).

Physics, like all the sciences, proves that man uses his brain only to the extent that it serves him, and it proves that the brain does not dominate man's knowledge of himself and his environment. Physics, like all the sciences, is the outcome of a working of the self, its intellect, which the self has recognized in itself and educated functionally by letting it do what it needed to develop its working—as it did with DNA at conception, with the brain as it was made, with perception after birth, and so on.

However, the intellect, like the brain, is only an instrument of the self; it has enormous possibilities but also considerable limitations. The most important one is that it is specialized and is not the whole self and all its possibilities. That is why, in addition to the sciences, there are the arts, music, and the dance, religious experience, the worlds of literature and of love, and the worlds still to be created.

## The Intellect in the Whole of the Self

No doubt the functioning of the self as an intellect has made it possible to know much that was unknown to the brain, and now the intellect is trying to know the brain intellectually and discover the full extent of the brain's capacity to help intellectual functioning because the brain has something the intellect has not yet managed to grasp: complexity.

The intellect has developed analytic thinking, logic (the various logics), the so-called experimental method, and the scientific method, and through them, it has scored such resounding successes that it has fascinated some men, who called it Reason, worshipped it, and took it away from the functionings of the intellect (thereby generating tension in the selves of the scientists who asked: "Has Reason surreptitiously brought Theology back into the sciences?"). This epoch of worship and anxiety was called "the Enlightenment." It demonstrated that man's mind is more than intellect, and since that period a more complex approach to the mind has been developed to account for the impact of affectivity upon the intellect. Today we go even further and consider the role of the "make-up" of the individual (that is, the soma and the brain) upon his thinking.

The epoch of the identification of the self with reason or the intellect is over, but since it was possible for men to believe that the self was at its best when it identified itself with the intellect, we have to accept as one of the functionings of the self a state in which part of the self can occupy the whole of consciousness. The intellect could achieve this and feel justified in achieving it, and the "elite" accepted the identification. This fact can guide us in understanding other identifications of the self with only one of its parts (and thereby provide the student of evolution with a new light to examine his subject).

## 9 The Intellectual Self

It has been possible for men to dwell in the intellect (and it still is), to develop views of the world from outside, and to be convinced that each is the total view. This delusion is a functioning of the self, whose contribution to the intellectual study of the self, co-extensive with all the sciences, can also give us the means of establishing a general theory of relativity in the field of knowing.

The self can identify with any of its parts or functionings.

The self can identify with perception and a certain amount of action, thus integrating somatic functionings that together permit a spectrum of lives. Those who dwell in these parts of the self make themselves sensitive to phenomena that escape others, and their contributions form the sciences of the occult.

The self can identify with action, subordinating perception and exalting the functionings of the soma that serve action, which produces the lives of all those men and women of action who fill the ranks of the sporting, military, and commercial worlds.

The self can identify with the realm of its feelings, either ignoring other functionings or using them instrumentally, thus producing the romantics, the explorers of love, the insane bent on living passion exclusively in any from, the explorers of the frontiers of experience through drugs or other means known to the self, the reformers of all kinds.

The self can identify with social action and hold that all the rest of the self gains its reality because of heredity. Social workers, a good proportion of politicians, men and women who go to form the bureaucracies, are examples of the lives that exalt this identification.

In these examples, the identification of the self with part of itself is reached intellectually, but in actual living it results from the individual functioning of the self and the opportunity (offered by complexity) to consume a life in making explicit the contents of that functioning. The self's identification with only a part of itself not only makes specialization possible but also makes it appear necessary. It makes each life unique in space-time, a constellation of mutually compatible behaviors and events in which the self as such is forgotten.

For the believer in God, to be able to forget God seems a paradox. For the person who knows the all-pervasive presence of the self, to be able to forget the self and stress only part of it is a functioning of the self, paradoxical only when general relativity is ignored.

Each of the places where the self can dwell becomes a brilliant palace, full of attractions, precisely because the self is such a tremendous sight that it enhances everything it dwells in. There is so much to find out that one life seems barely sufficient. Hence, the self mobilizes everything to serve the end of identification. The mobilization itself is not part of one's interest, only what it can do in the service of the identification. Every life, every biography, shows one of the possibilities available. The process it self makes the number of these possibilities infinite.

## 9 The Intellectual Self

When Reason was identified as a deity in the intellect, this assertion actually brought the germ that could destroy the scientist's identification with the light that biased his view of the world. For the worship of Reason made the scientist irrational. Instead of ensuring the predominance of the intellect, it opened the door to the whole self and to the possibility of limiting the working of the intellect to intellectual matters, although Reason wanted the whole universe. It could have the whole universe of intellectual experience. But irrational Reason claimed that there was nothing beyond it and that the universe of the intellect was <u>the</u> universe.

A succession of mental blows experienced by the scientist within his own science forced him to abandon that claim, or be considered insane. The intellectual self came to acknowledge that it was only one of the self's modalities of being, that specialization was an unfortunate limitation even for the workings of the intellect, that many of the insoluble problems that the intellectual self faced were due to its ways of working, that the problems might disappear if other parts of the self, other methods of facing reality, were allowed in.

Early in this century quantum mechanics and relativity theory were considered to be huge feats of the intellect <u>and</u> the burial places of intellectualism and Reason. They were found entirely by the intellect of Planck and Einstein, who looked inside themselves and not at nature, and so these achievements could only boost the prestige of the intellect. But they made man revise the neat constructs of previous generations, they created many paradoxes and baffled the minds of the followers, the worshippers, of Reason. Accepting axioms instead of truths became the attitude of the scientist, who thus withdrew from the world of experiments and entered the world of experiencing.

Science today is as vast as experience. To be a scientist is no longer to belong to the club of those who adore Reason but simply to be an alert investigator of what strikes one's fancy, only watchful that one does not deceive oneself.

The intellectual self has now found a place in the whole self, instead of occupying all the space. Its place is a place of honor, since it has special far-reaching powers that still produce some remarkable feat every day, even if it is somewhat subdued by the spectacle of what it has seen by peeping outside its boundaries.

# III

# The Mind Always Educates the Brain

# 10  The Sensitive Self

To account for the ability of the self to perceive what goes on in the soma, it has been necessary to consider a proprioceptive sense, in addition of course to the sense organs that relate to the outside world. Elsewhere we suggested that a "sense of truth" is necessary to account for perceiving reality in experience. No doubt a "sense of rhythm," a "sense of proportion," a "common sense" are also often required to make sense of experience.

Awareness as a general property of the self is all-pervasive, like the self. But since awareness does not have the property of objectifying itself, it operates entirely within the self and its manifestations. Awareness is the agent of the self that informs it of the existence of anything and maintains the presence of this thing within the conscious self. <u>Sensitivity</u> is the name we shall give to any of awareness's way of workings that the self can be aware of, and we shall distinguish sensitivities from each other by the particular content of the self that dwells in each type of awareness.

## Sensitivity, Vulnerability, and Their Uses

The self is capable of adding sensitivities to its endowment by making itself vulnerable to some functioning of itself, by making itself aware of the existence of such an opening and cultivating it. Vulnerability is an active movement of the self, permitting some kind of energy change to be noted and a flow of energy to be maintained. This capacity we shall describe as <u>dwelling in.</u> Awareness is required for noting, but vulnerability results from maintaining the presence of the self, or awareness, in what was noted.

A sensitivity works properly only if the presence of awareness is solely concerned with the dynamics of what has been (or is being) noted. The dynamics of the self can of course intervene in the working of any sensitivity and can qualify or replace its capacity to take note by entertaining what is concomitant but irrelevant to its working. The self can also maintain the presence of a sensitivity with care, watch for interferences, and stop them.

The self needs many sensitivities to cope with the simultaneous functionings of itself in the complex of objectified and free energy and the aggressions from the environment. The self, in its elementary and permanent way of being, creates sensitivities as soon as the need appears.

The sense of truth is one of the self's sensitivities and is made available to the self from the start, so that it can tell the self, for example, that magnesium must be integrated with some protein to produce the hemoglobin for the blood or other such pinpointed re-cognitions that are later passed on to the brain for automatic survey and maintenance. The sense of truth accompanies every perception so that the self knows the perception, while the brain can add the perception to its store in the form of energy (recognizable at the cosmic level by the objectifications which are akin to it). For example, photons are known by the self, and the sense of truth confirms them by recognizing that the eye or the skin receives the inputs of energy. The sense of truth is the arbiter of the truth in an experience, leaving to other senses the processing of the input.

People called "sensitives," mediums, and the like, know of their uncommon powers through their sense of truth, even if many observers are not convinced. But their sense of truth is not their special power. Rather, their power is a vulnerability that they have cultivated, a special presence of their self in one of their functionings. We shall discuss "sensitives" in more detail below.

Sensitivity, as awareness, can be aware of itself, sensitive to itself. Therefore, it is educable. All of us educate scores of sensitivities during our lives, which make us alert to often minute changes in the complexion of the self.

Thus, we can make ourselves vulnerable to <u>double entendre</u>, to irony, to puns, to humor, to flat notes, to color contrasts, to the beauty of someone's teeth, to hypocrisy, to moral integrity, to the presence of others, and so on.

Sometimes we can educate our brain to pick up shades of presence, as we can for color contrast, smells, notes. In other instances, the brain is involved only marginally, and it influences the activity of the self by generating a network of mental patterns that can be kept going by an energy loop. For example, in the field of mathematics the self can educate the brain to function in such a way as to scan for arithmetical inconsistencies. In the field of language, to scan for grammatical errors. In the field of tennis, for possible responses to adversary. Similarly in poker.

Any survey of fifty years of work in a field of study will show many sensitivities grasping some element in the field and becoming more sensitive to its proper meaning—to its relative significance to the whole, to its capacity sometimes to grow in importance and significance and possibly dominate the scene and perform a renewal of the study, or simply to distract because of its attractiveness, its ease of handling, and perhaps even its alien associations that favor a current bias. This collective display of involvements coincides with individual choices of using one sensitivity rather than another and the co-presence of so many sensitivities that can be compatible with each other and can affect each other.

The self, in addition to having a store of possibilities of making itself repeatedly vulnerable, also owns the ability to replace a set of initially distinguishable sensitivities by a wider sensitivity that integrates the others, making them work better and illuminate each other.

Without these dynamics no one could master the use of a historically developed complex language. And the fact that synthesizing is done so early in life vouches for the fact that it is a property of the self that is easily accessible and educable by awareness.

If such a sensitivity is passed to the brain as a functioning that requires little supervision by the self, it becomes part of the person's make-up, usable in all circumstances. It joins the background of the person's intelligent behaviors and gives the person access to the results of synthetic vision.

Vulnerability is needed to enter a new field, sensitivity is needed to know what goes on in it, to remain engaged in some of its aspects. Sensitivity of that sensitivity will make the self clear the ground of other conscious involvements and will reduce the contact with other impacts while enhancing those required for the new demands accepted by the self. What happens in sleep does not necessarily follow the same pattern.

## The Sensitivity of Sensitives

The study of "sensitives" illustrates all of the above very well. There are sensitives in all realms. Once they recognize their vulnerability they are able to become more and more sensitive to components of their chosen realm and to achieve what appears to the non-educated in that field to be feats, incredible performances, assurance in front of danger, readiness to consider behaviors so dangerous that even simple errors could be fatal.

## III
### The Mind Always Educates the Brain

Sensitives in the molecular field can become prospectors, diviners, radiesthetists. All of them seem to be endowed with exceptional powers, although they are only normal people who have enhanced a possibility present in every self to become vulnerable to one aspect of their self, the maker of their soma. They have the more or less unique feature of giving themselves to a specialized relationship between the self and its molecules.

Even if they cannot articulate the way they reach a sensitivity to the various atomic impulses that emanate from certain objects, through carefully arranged experiments they and others can find that, indeed, something in the sensitives is "upset" by the presence of these impulses.

The role of such an experiment is to satisfy the incredulous, to add to the collection of facts. It rarely provides understanding. To reach this we need to go back to the self, its objectifications and its presence in them. The sensitive who can manifest himself by describing what he experiences in some circumstances—who recognizes his "upset"—is the same self who works at the verbal and social levels through speech and at the molecular and vital through his soma. He has to be aware, at the level of the phenomenon, how to be "upset" in a very special way, and then to know through his sense of truth that indeed the "upset" is generated by certain circumstances, and only then can he assert it verbally to friends or to anyone else. The instrument in his investigation is awareness of changes in the soma, and therefore in the self. It seems absurd to grant the right to a man-made instrument such as a voltmeter to be "upset" by the presence of "volts" in itself and deny the same right to a sensitive when he is "upset" by what happens to himself and is equipped to deal with it!

The soma _is_ molecular, cellular, vital. It took months to prepare the instruments in it to cope with the three realms in which it lives. This means that the self has delegated to some organs and some functionings the delicate tasks of deciding the level at which an impact is acceptable and is safe, and to react by taking steps to cope with an impact that exceeds the acceptable level. Observers can see that many of these reactions need to work well in order to reject harmful impacts. But the mechanism of judging the quality of the impact precedes the act of response. The soma, and hence the self, must know itself well enough to dub a particular impact as pernicious or indifferent or favorable and then move towards rejection or tolerance or integration.

The work of sensitives in their special fields may differ from their ordinary coping with external impacts in that the energy that "upsets" them is minute in amount compared with an impact that would trigger an ordinary reaction. But the nature of the impact is the same. The impact's quantity, which the self recognizes before recognizing the quality, is acknowledged by the respondent in his soma and amplified by the brain (or those part of the brain that are part of the amplifying system), so that the self has no doubt what the impact is. If the self can verbalize the assessment, others can be apprised of it. No one can dispute that each blue photon is blue independently of the intensity of the blue light impinging on the retina.

These sensitives operate at the total human level in response to what happens to them at the molecular or vital level. They can therefore judge how to label the impact they are experiencing and can recommend actions that are related to what they have put themselves in touch with. Thus, they can ask for wells to be dug at certain spots to certain depths to reach water in the soil, or to find oil or minerals or even corpses, treasures, etc. Only their reputation is at stake in repeated failure or success, and not the phenomena of sensitivity nor the functionings that have led them to even one finding.

To understand the existence of sensitives only requires that one recognize an awareness of sensitivity to cosmic forces and to their presence in amounts sufficient to upset molecular behaviors in the soma so that they can be noticed. To such occurrences we are all submitted every day several times, and we take in our stride the fact that we are competent, normally, to respond to them.

## The Sensitivity of "Ordinaries"

We can enhance or dampen the desire for food, smoking, or flattery. If we specialize in the observation of such phenomena, we can understand the way that anyone can relate the fine dynamics of awareness of somatic changes to sources in the universe and can enhance their awareness by this attention.

We can educate ourselves to become more and more sensitive in selected areas. We only need to see that we all have many choices open to us, and although we may not have given ourselves to this or that, others have. Our incredulity that some people can do what we have never attempted and even do it easily, is a fault in our exposure to the possibilities of the self. If some of us can educate ourselves to become virtuosos in the use of a musical instrument, how can we deny that similar feats are open to those who specialize in working on the trapeze, in training wild beasts, in hearing beyond the ordinary range of sounds, in seeing beyond what meets the eye, and so on?

A sensitive physician trusts his capacity to reach the causes beyond symptoms. A sensitive counselor has made himself vulnerable to what prompts people to come out with certain statements and pursues that reality rather than the obvious clues.

A sensitive spouse may be doing the right thing by simply enhancing the presence of the other in his or her awareness and the presence of love.

A sensitive parent may let all that has gone to form knowledge of the child into his or her consciousness so as to meet the child in the present circumstances and illumine the conduct that generates some action or reaction.

A sensitive writer may relate to the language he uses, not only for expression, but for the "best" expression that takes account of his own aesthetic standards. The working out of each sentence can be as easy as locating a well is for a dowser or as demanding as the delivery of a baby, but it is invisible after the sentence is written down.

Each of us can be said to spend his life cultivating sensitivities and reaching more of ourselves by letting our sensitivities expose us to more of the complexities of our universes.

The functions of the sensitive self are part of all our awarenesses, but the functions do not stop there, for we can give ourselves to our sensitivities. In particular we can give ourselves to the study of our sensitivities and of our sensitivity as one aspect of the self, and become specially sensitive to sensitivity. According to how much we manage this, our life becomes open, making us vulnerable to all sorts of movements of the spirit in us and more capable of meeting complexity, respecting it by not forcing it into the forms that suit our limitations, and learning from it that the self's own complexity prepares us for the act of knowing what is as it is. Often men and women confuse "what is" with what "should be." A special sensitivity to "shoulds" is needed to maintain the self in contact with the whole of reality.

## The Social uses of Sensitivity

It is possible to recast the history of mankind in terms of sensitivity. Only when one or more people have made themselves vulnerable to a certain reality does this reality take its place in our lives, in Reality. Today, we are becoming individually and collectively sensitive to the meaning of the person in each of us and to constructing a world that can work smoothly while preserving the uniqueness of each of us.

Only a little more than a century ago did society begin to create social institutions and express itself as a community collectively taking care of the needs of groups and individuals. Around 1850, in the West, sociology was created and became more important each decade, attracting people who were sensitive to the dynamics of that universe of social relations and to related fields of study that each displayed a sensitivity to a particular challenge. Sociology, anthropology, ethnology, ethnography, demography, etc., are signs of the subtly differentiated sensitivities that have given themselves to deeper, and therefore more distinguishable, areas of vulnerability.

Two centuries earlier, around 1650, natural history became the preoccupation of many people who were sensitive to the content of nature and vulnerable to the differences and similarities that made possible the flourishing of the natural and exact sciences: botany, zoology, geology, cosmography, microscopy, physics, chemistry, anatomy, physiology, etc.

The sciences are a way mankind has found to educate its members about the tenets of Reality. Once one person has shown that he was vulnerable to a certain reality and could become more and more sensitive to that reality, a collectivity follows that produces the joint awarenesses that are available for the use and growth of everyone. Facts cannot gain the name of facts before someone becomes aware of their existence and devotes himself to their study.

Now study is not the work of sensitivity, but it is a proof that sensitivity is at work as a steady presence of the self and its endowments, maintaining vulnerability to the particular reality that the student is linked to.

Sensitivity is required of each of us all through life simply because it is the way the self notes what is and what is happening to itself. The <u>study</u> of sensitivity is not required, but if we engage in it, we find one or more realities to give ourselves to. If we give ourselves to the reality of being sensitive to sensitivity, then many worlds open up and life cannot but be abundant. This is one of the possibilities of a self that has made itself expert in the cognition and recognition of what comes its way, selecting out what is of interest to itself and, sometimes, to others.

Very few Greeks heeded when Socrates became aware of consciousness and its tremendous power to produce a more human world. But when Descartes found that he was a thinking being, many others followed suit, and modern science became possible.

Montaigne discovered the universe of the self and its importance for all living, but his words remained only as rare echoes punctuating European culture in the works of Pascal, Rousseau, and Stendhal, which were heard against the flow of chatter of the Cartesian and Baconian disciples. The Romantics in all countries, aware of the sentimental self, studied sentimental sensitivity and kept alive the works of Montaigne, Pascal, and others, but did not fully give themselves to their message.

Literary fashions are useful threads to follow in the study of individual and collective vulnerability and sensitivity. Each literary work of art tells us what matters to the author, but because it is published, purchased, kept on shelves in libraries, it also speaks of the sensitivity of other people who respond to the work.

Because of our more conscious interest in sensitivity today, we are learning to take each sensitivity where it is on the spectrum and not brush it away to cultivate our own hobby. The present, still groping for methods that will permit a full study of the whole field, is gradually learning tolerance for what has been neglected but is as scientific as other scientific endeavors. The study of sensitives and their universes is one example. Tolerance can, of course, go with indifference. Only the active participation of many diverse investigators can change an occult field into an honorable science.

The self uses sensitivity for the study of sensitivity, and we are moving towards a body of knowledge in this direction that can constitute many branches of the overall science of man. A creation of a group of sciences is always a forerunner of a new civilization. The science of man makes an "Earthian" society possible just as the creation of social studies assumed the existence of local societies and intellectual studies the existence of universal reason.

The learning phase for the pioneers, which corresponds to meeting the new, the yet unknown, leads to so-called "intuitive" but inspiring works. The learning phase for the consolidators, the multitude of contributors who survey wide and large and occasionally deeply in the field that already is opened up for them, leads to the established science. This phase can work itself to death, into routine and trivial research, unless the third phase of learning shows itself: the use of the learner's self as he has been able to make himself so as to enter a new world once more.

## Sensitivity, the Brain, and the Study of Sensitivity

The work of the "sensitives" and "the brain" go hand in hand. The first presents the extraordinary in terms of a model of what each of us can do; the second, in its complexity, offers the suggestion that it holds the secret of the first and may perhaps not require us to renew ourselves. In fact, the two challenges can be compounded and do not cancel each other.

We may need the sensitives' awareness of themselves to develop the true instrument for the study of the brain beyond the naive anatomical concept of complexity. If sensitivity covers all the manifestations of the self, the brain can come in only because it is more than anatomy, more than physiology: it is connected to the self through mental functionings. These can be studied somatically but without necessarily yielding a specific location in the brain. They may be possible because of what the brain offers the self, but be objectified in the world of action, or insight, or relationships, and not in the brain.

Perhaps the sensitives who will permit a breakthrough in our understanding do not operate at the molecular or vital levels. For there are sensitives in all fields of manifestation, and we need to know them all to assert that we have studied the whole field of sensitivity.

Only those who use imagination can tell us what it is; only lovers can competently speak of love; only friends of friendships. Only those sensitive to the reality of time will say something worthwhile about it; only those sensitive to ethics, how and why morality exists in us.

Only those vulnerable to sensitivity as such, and not to one or other of its manifestations, will give themselves to the search for the "instruments" that will make its functionings obvious. Those who devote themselves to the study of sensitivity—and I count myself among them—may come up with insights that can be shared by others.

Earlier, in Chapter 3, I referred to my experiments with a special instrument that recorded energy changes in people. My purpose in these experiments was to track in others what my sensitivity had suggested to me. I call it a "Gayograph" because it was Alphonse Gay who made it and put it in my hands. At the time I first became acquainted with it (in 1951), I knew it was susceptible of being "upset" by some of the manifestations of the self as expressed through energy variations in the soma. Since then I have found that it not only can do that but also can serve as a probe to follow precisely any aspects of the self that use the soma and yet take place in the mind or in the self.

While EEG, brain surgery, and brain explorations want to give a somatic origin to all man's manifestations, even an origin in the brain, the Gayograph makes it possible to go straight to the energy—free or locked in the tissues—and learn about its vicissitudes. The Gayograph allows a human exploration of human beings. If some manifestations are found to be linked to the nervous system, this connection will be an additional attribute not the essential property of the manifestations.

The instrument has two parts. The first is a mechanical probe attached to the skin at a point (say, the tibia) where the probe can be affected by what goes on between (and perhaps in or along) a bone and the skin. The second part is a means of showing the variation of this reality over time on a meter, which can be recorded in the form of a trace.

With this instrument we now know:

1. how to follow what the self does to its energy all the time;

2. that the free energy of the self is present everywhere in the soma and that its effects on the surface of the bag (the skin) can be made evident on the probe of the instrument;

3. that free energy displays a temporary structuration involving minute amounts of energy coagulated by the slightest expression of the self: a thought, a mood, an emotion, an activation of a functioning;

4. that different people, besides displaying idiosyncratic characteristics, can also display a common affectation of energy, paralleling what can be gathered through language, and classifiable as collective behaviors;

5   that this mechanical probe can reach all the features of the state of the self that EEG or other instruments can reach—particularly in the case of epilepsy, it can study the brain center and its exalted activity just as easily, if not more easily;

6   that a Gayogram can make visible the physiognomy of an "aggression" upon the self and allows one to examine it pin-pointedly for its components, thus yielding information otherwise inaccessible—for example, the kind of "upset" experienced by a sensitive;

7   that the presence of the self in the soma displays "laterality"—that is, that two probes, one on each tibia, consistently produce tracings that display differing amplitudes on each side and of the same order for all phenomena (in addition to specific features concerned with the person an the special activity of the self at that time);

8   that the details of the pulses as they are accessible to trained Chinese workers can be displayed as faithfully and as completely on a tracing (the difference is only that the Chinese scholar is sensitive to his sensitivity but the instrument is sensitive only to the energy vicissitudes, and the traces require interpretation to understand what they say about the behavior of the artery);

9   that the energy changes accompanying a change in the state of the self can be spotted as they occur, and that properties of the self at work on intellectual matters can be as easily studied as the formation of images, the evocation of scenes or people, the presence of verbalization in a subject

while he seems to be concentrating on a visual task, or of affectivity when verbalizing;

10  that we can distinguish functionings that correspond to different energy budgets in the self and establish a hierarchy of these functionings in terms of energy consumption and efficiency—the intellect, for example, seems to use very little energy in activities that do not evoke emotions and to use it selectively;

11  that synthetic movements of the mind can be analyzed in terms of energy and that it seems possible one day to reach the energy distribution in the recorded tracing of the imagery, the emotions, the thoughts, the virtual actions, etc.;

12  that the fine somatic adjustments required by the use of the soma switching from speaking one language to another can be closely followed and inform us about the connections between skills and somatic structures and the effects on them of linguistic components;

13  that we can separate mental activities from the activity of the brain, remain in contact with the vicissitudes of the first as the mind can and not involve the brain more than its contributions make necessary in the field where it has been educated;

14  that the instrument corresponds to our level of awareness and lets us study the self directly in its dynamics and functionings within the soma, that is, as unlocked energy, and because of that to find the domain of the brain in man's life.

All the above is clearly the outcome of sensitivity being aware of itself. When it knows itself through other components of the self, these efforts bring in the instruments of the different components and the intellectual theories that correspond to them. Thus, in the direct study of sensitivity, the brain is secondary, but it may become the center or the conditioner of progress in understanding sensitivity if we move through the intellect.

## The Sensitive Self and the Unknown

If a sensitive self exists, it is to this sensitivity that we shall leave the knowledge of itself. If the self can consider sensitivity as knowable, the self will propose the means to know it. Without such self awareness, there can only be a collection of curiosities in the field, as in the books proclaiming the world of the occult or in publications reporting "extra-ordinary" phenomena.

These curiosities are evidence of a manifestation of the self that is immanent and that will become "natural" as soon as the self gives itself the instruments to render visible what can be reached by self awareness.

Intuition is the way of knowing the immanent.

Intuition can become a sensitivity if it is applied steadily to some objectified aspect of the immanent, which then joins the ranks of the known, the real, the common place.

## III
### The Mind Always Educates the Brain

Descartes knew that <u>he</u> needed intuition to establish Reason as an instrument among the instruments that theologians used to penetrate the world of creatures. He was a "sensitive" in his time, for he could not refer to the evidence accumulated by centuries of work after him. When enough people had become "sensitized" to the reality he intuited, there was no need for a special gift to enter his world; education was sufficient.

Intellectualists of all kinds must sensitize themselves in order to operate on those manifestations of the intellect that are distinguishable only for the initiated. Scientists are differently sensitized to work in chemistry, physics, biology, and so forth, and the education of their sensitivity is visible in the swiftness with which they notice the opportunities their field offers their mind.

But sensitives remain bound to special functionings of the mind; this connections limits their receptivity to opportunities in other fields, and they can blunt their sensitivity to their errors when they reduce the world of reality to what they comprehend. Thus, although scientists know that ears hear and eyes see, they seem not to understand that some new sensitivity may be needed before they can entertain phenomena that are classed among the occult. They dare to patronize the study of the world and demand that all reality be bent to penetrate their minds through the sensitivities <u>they</u> have developed.

Speaking for myself, I have had to renew myself every time I have had the chance of encountering a challenge for which I had some entry in my endowments. I have let the challenge educate me, and I have become a student of it.

My sensitivity told me that since the brain was only part of the soma, and since it did not seem to know itself, I had to endeavor to find out how I would know the brain, my brain, through that component in me that knew itself.

Looking at the proposals made by students of the brain, it is clear that they expect that a sensitivity to the full complexity of the brain will one day emerge in one brain and that this future event will lead to its full understanding.

It seems more appropriate to become sensitive to the knower in oneself and to follow knowing from conception to rebirth and to be in contact with what we have to do with every power of the self. These powers include the brain, no doubt; but much more. They include, in particular, that which makes the brain contribute its powers to grasping the immanent and that integrates the brain in the various selves around.

To this end we can devote vulnerability, the necessary, preliminary movement to develop sensitivity.

# 11 The Relating Self

The component of objectification and the component of perceiving an outer world together produce realities for the self that generate a world of being, the world of relationships.

To relate to oneself is a life-long functioning, with any number of variations resulting from self awareness. To relate to what is not oneself additionally demands that the self (1) knows what can be relied on because it can find a way of being that takes care of future changes and (2) knows what has the built-in freedom of not being previsible, has a will to transform itself beyond recognition.

Into these three universes—of ourselves, of what can be relied on that is not ourselves, and of what is unknown—fall most of the happenings in our lives, even though they can mutually affect each other and can present an infinitely renewable universe of experiencing to the self that can be known as a unity.

A failure to recognize the existence of these three universes causes much of the confusion that can make life for some of us far less abundant than for those who have deliberately learned to be with the universes and their respective realities.

To conceive of the unknown as being known by someone, or the previsible as being the full fabric of reality, is a mistake that some people entertain because they have woven a way of thinking that tends to want to reproduce a particular state of affairs everywhere.

If the mistake is not spotted and if such thinking is maintained and nourished, it can lead to a <u>sui generis</u> way of relating, fraught with danger to one's sanity. This is so simply because the universe is outside our control, and it can, and does, challenge us in its own ways.

There are elements that make each day, meteorologically and cosmographically, unique. And this uniqueness can be noted. Nevertheless, we alternatively can relate to that which makes every day appear as just another day, and we can know only what is as previsible as the rising and setting of the sun.

We relate to people in this way, at least to some of them, wanting them to be predictable and engaged in living in a way that does not startle or jolt <u>us</u>. We allow these people to be themselves only if being themselves means that they are what we expect of them.

## Relating to Ourselves

Since each of us lives with the instrumental past, exploring the present and letting the unknown future find its way in us, relating to our self at each moment is by itself complex. Our inability to be fully alert, fully conscious, aware of everything all at the same time, brings in uncertainties that lead us to meet what comes our way with improvised approaches that may not always work. For instance, we can accept views of ourselves held by superficial observers, unfriendly judges, or uninterested relatives.

Only exceptionally can we relate to ourselves so that we are always ourselves, for a number of reasons. First, we are born in an environment that is outside our control. We cannot make it serve our view of the world at every moment, particularly since we change our needs and purposes all the time and no one else is really able to know them, or is even interested in knowing them. Second, our own grasp of life is always idiosyncratic and only guesswork can provide it. With guesswork goes errors and uncertainty. Third, others in the environment have their own lives to attend to. Fourth, and most important, what we do over the twenty-four hours of each day, every day, in sleep and the waking state, is the light that must guide us and will lead to the most realistic view of ourselves, however distorted that may be. To be oneself in all these circumstances cannot but be very difficult.

Still, the human environment relates to the newborn child by giving it time and elementary assistance (food, shelter, and some care), without interference. Interference begins later, in the form of reactions to the child's demands if they are not at once akin to what the family knows how to provide. Babies then have opportunities to learn the various meanings of relationship to various people, at various moments, in various circumstances.

The perceptions of others in their relation to the self are matters of fact and subject to doubt only if the others are erratic, unpredictable. Then the self may wish for particular responses rather than those which come. But on the whole, the responses are predictable, even if they are not helpful, and no sense of doubt is generated, only a uniform response to uniform behaviors.

From these perceptions of others, we can generate a component of our perception of ourselves, also a matter of fact, as far as the environment tells us how we appear to it.

## Relating to the Environment

Whenever the work we have to do by ourselves is permitted to go on, the environment has little effect on us. But sometimes the dynamics in the environment prevent us from taking good care of ourselves by denying us the exercises that are vital to us at that level. For instance, if we have to be quiet for a long time because of some illness in the home; or if we cannot keep anything to play with because of a bully of a brother; or if we must not make ourselves dirty because Mom wants us to be model children; or, more commonly, if we do not have certain facilities in our home because life has been hard on our parents.

The impact of the environment can be canceled or enhanced by the working of the self, and this, too, contributes to how we relate to ourselves and to others. According to what we bring with us to life, we can use the resources of the self to learn what to do to cope with aggressions and what to do to take advantage of opportunities. We cannot only react, putting into our reaction the action directly opposite to the one that affects us, we can also respond by absorbing what is absorbable and imaginatively considering what is left. There are some children who can charm their siblings and disarm all aggressors, who can get away with anything.

It is commonly assumed that the environment plays a considerable role in shaping us, but it is not as commonly held that we can also stand up to tremendous pressures in the environment and neutralize their effects.

The self is very resilient, for it knows how to work with what is given and how to work at the local level to meet the here and now. It may be only a superficial view that would see us as easy prey and targets for aggressions from all directions. The self knows how to open up and shut off, to stress and ignore, to enhance and diminish, to entertain or dropout. To retreat into sleep, into one's bag and what happens within it, is everyone's privilege.

This makes relating a human activity that involves choices and degrees, everything or nothing or anything in between.

Hence, there is some learning for us to pursue all the time in the field of relating, and the self that makes its own selections manifests its responsibility simply by its response.

To relate to music in a concert hall may mean to surrender to it. To relate to a description of a physics experiment in a treatise may mean the cautious reading of each word, the formation of intricate images shot through with the specially trained sensitivity that is used in this area, organizing the resulting intellectual construct so that it agrees with one's intuition of the phenomenon and the consistency of other physical phenomena.

To relate to a fairy tale may be to accept that anything is permissible so long as the tale respects the logic of fantasy, meaning that no arbitrary components are allowed to distract the imagination.

To relate to a picture on the wall may be to let one's sight receive the overall impact of line and color that generates a climate and to use one's ocular muscles to scan the area of the canvas analytically and one's focusing powers to note details, enhancing some feelings and letting relevant experiences merge with all of this.

To relate to food may be to let one's appetite, one's perception of smell and appearance, one's previous experiences, one's built-in habits (resulting from cultural or familial traditions), all merge together to trigger the actions of eating and enjoying, or of rejection.

To relate to tools, or to learn the rules of a game, may mean to accept the likelihood of making mistakes, to try again, to pay in some predetermined fashion when the performance does not reach a particular level, to be persistent, and to develop proper behaviors.

And these are only a few of the ways we relate to the given, all different, all using what we are and what we have. In these responses we do not necessarily end up as one of the many available simplistic stereotypes depicting man in his environment, stereotypes that serve no one.

Even if the brain is needed to make all these relatings possible, it certainly plays only a part, a minor part, in the elaboration of the shaded relationships that the self finds itself capable of creating and knowing.

Clearly the conditions for being able to play marbles are somatic, and the brain must function in certain ways before a player can enter the game. But the coordination of particular uses of hand and eye is the action of the self, which all along judges progress and how the brain must be used in order to hold the newly acquired competence. The self <u>makes</u> this new functioning of the brain.

## Relating to Others

In relating to other people, and to oneself in those relationships, there are many things to learn, particularly the truth that all of us are unpredictable, moody, unclear about ourselves, manipulated by habits and unconscious movements, the plaything of ideas and ideals, and so on.

We have to learn to enhance concern, which is a feeling that is foreshadowed in the self and the brain in the ability to take care of the somatic dysfunctions immediately.

We have to learn to keep in our minds images of those we relate to, images of enough plasticity so that we not only experience their presence but also give them the freedom that is compatible with their reality.

We have to learn to be watchful of the signs that inform us about a relationship; whether all is well and things can go on as before or, on the contrary, whether an invisible boundary has been trespassed and an adjustment is required here and now; whether we must guess how to behave in the circumstances; and so on.

We have to distinguish between a vast number of possible relationships which structure our social world, our community, and develop for each a set of distinct behaviors and dynamics.

These sets of behaviors are sometimes interchangeable, sometimes rigidly adhered to, and the learner has to discover what makes this the way it is. The unknown social position of a person known to a child may affect his elders' behaviors in a mysterious way and create confusion over the criteria that the child may use. Someone who was a comparative stranger can suddenly become a close relative by marriage, and adjustments in the relationship will be needed.

In the field of love relations, there are other things to learn. What does one do with jealousy, possessiveness? How much care, excitement, attraction, can one display in differing circumstances?

What are steady and durable relationships? What are the special demands of these relationships, and why are they not a part of simple, casual relationships?

Can one ever be oneself in a relationship?

With this question, a world opens up at once.

If one knows an upsurge of sensuality in the presence of another person, is it being oneself in a relationship to give expression to it or, on the contrary, is it only relating to one's inner movements?

What does being a member of a couple mean in terms of its additions to oneself and its control of what one is when the other member is not present?

What are the realities of various kinds of couples when one takes into account love, social ties, family ties, social taboos, etc.? Can we consider father and child to be capable of some intimacies in the world of feelings, interests, companionships, that make a unique couple out of the two, affecting both as much as, or even more than, the members of an another kind of couple are affected by intimacies that involve sensual or sexual appetites?

What is forgiveness, and what are legitimate expectations in certain relationships involving oneself? What makes for truly mutual connections? What is consent? tacit consent? acceptance as a matter of course? What is negotiable in a true relationship? Or is there anything negotiable to begin with? Is freedom to be reserved or handed out?

What is the basis of trust in a relationship? Can a relationship be true in spite of a lack of trust? Can we relate and yet be suspicious?

If watchfulness over oneself is required in order to avoid hurting others, should that watchfulness be applied to the other, or would this jeopardize the relationship (for perhaps watchfulness cannot function at the same time as complete trust)?

What sorts of tests met in life will maintain some of the true features of relationships? What is betrayal? What behaviors by another are compatible with feelings generated in oneself by the other?

How does one manage to know someone other than oneself? Is it entirely precluded by the nature of individuality? Must one know oneself to a certain level before one can expect to know someone else? Is love itself a way of knowing that does not need any other way? Must we reconcile various ways of knowing to experience the benefits of love fully?

How is it that people who have been intimate can become strangers? Is this the opposite movement to strangers becoming intimate or something utterly different?

How is it that not everyone can become a member of a couple? Or does everyone in fact become such a member?

Is the appetite that leads one person towards another linked to one's body-image? Or to some illusion that occupies the mind? Or to something purely animal, a degenerate relationship, lived only at one level?

How is it that people can find infinite satisfaction in each other, constant renewal in each other's presence? What serves the self as a basis for such a relationship, longed for by everyone yet only rarely actualized?

Can education of the awareness of oneself and of one's perception of a person produce the realization of the ideal couple? Or does it lead to universal love?

Is universal love a reality? An ideal? An illusion? A projection by the intellect of a process that is valid in some areas of the realm of relationship?

Is universal love desirable? By whom? Why?

What is the difference between longing and appetite, greed and possession?

What is passion? What place does it have in our life, in life's various manifestations?

Can one educate oneself to reach all that is required by the numerous relationships one can be involved in and objectify each relationship selectively so as to be true to its components? Is there a technology of relationship? Or is technology inevitably excluded?

## The Realm of Relationship

No doubt the self in each of us lives through much of what we have itemized here in the form of questions. That we can ask all these questions says that the relating self has much to do in order to take care of this universe, a universe which cannot be reduced to any other nor to all the others put together. It is a realm for humans, as the universe of the vital is a realm for all plants. Each human may live in as much of this realm as he or she has made himself vulnerable to, and as much as he has managed to attain to, by his use of his time.

Because we cannot generate out of others, by a procedure as simple as algebra, say, the realm of relationship, we cannot give the jobs to be done to the brain. Like all the other co-present components, the brain has a role to play, and we can devise experiments that prove that there are places in the brain that can produce exaltation, calm, sexual arousal, the triggers and controllers of passion, dynamic images, and so forth. But the brain remains an instrument of the self, and only awareness can educate us to be as we need to be in each of the relationships we find ourselves in.

The relating self not only functions <u>sui generis</u>; it can, once it has developed enough of the realm of relationship, serve as a basis for the self's further adventures in new universes that require more than relationship.

# 12  The Moral Self

We have seen that the self finds a sense of truth in itself, a sense of its functionings and what needs to be done to relate more adequately to situations; we have seen the self finding intelligence at work, being vulnerable to many realms and to what goes on in them through any number of sensitivities. It can be claimed that some of these sensitivities belong to the modes of expression of some animals, and that they are linked with the evolution of the brain. But when we come to morality, we enter a strictly human universe, for the self must find its ethics in a universe that is three stages removed from the soma. Even if we find that we can speak of a "moral sense" in man, it is there in the way that we found the intellect or intelligence in man: a special awareness gives it its existence.

## The Baby and the Moral Sense

When the umbilical cord is cut immediately after birth, a baby's face shows all the signs of anger and indignation, and in his awareness of helplessness, he can only cry and shriek.

## III
### The Mind Always Educates the Brain

This reception into our midst gives the self the first experience of what it is like to be acted upon in a way that does not suit it, although it is aware that it has no control over what others do, particularly in regard to itself.

Because of the existence of this human universe of others, the self needs an alertness to shape the moral self as that aspect of the self that watches over intrusive experience with the proper sensitivities.

From birth onwards we are immersed in the intercourse of people whose idea of their own interest moves them to take actions that may be justified to themselves but not necessarily to others. The uncertainty that colors the motives of others, whatever the content of their actions, generates in everyone a state of mind that accepts a lack of clarity in these matters and produces the certainty that it is right to take up an egocentric position.

The fiber in the self that can be touched when its interests are at stake makes the self capable of actions and manifestations that belong to the universe of ethics. The capacity for indignation, shown as soon as we are born, marks the threshold of the special sensitivity that gives reality to one's moral sense and mobilizes the energy of the self in the special forms that belong to this universe.

The baby can find opportunities every day to note whether the environment (that indeterminate expanse of forces in the hands of other people) is concerned with his wellbeing. Are his needs attended to at once, in due time, or capriciously? Is he left in conditions of discomfort, in a tight garment, in a bad posture, wet, or under extremes of temperature in a breeze or in the sun? Is his crying responded to or ignored? Is he made to expend too much energy to get attention from the environment?

What his conclusions are we cannot say. But we cannot deny that babies can be aware of these relationships with the environment and learn from them a number of ways of judging it—at least, to judge with criteria based on self-interest and concrete data. So it is possible for observers of babies to find that the attitudes towards the self in relation to the environment may be formed very early, even though social dynamics are of course still transcendental for babies.

A child who becomes shy and develops a capacity to put up with a lot of aggression and sets a very high threshold for his indignation, displays one possible ethical attitude. Another child who engages in socially disruptive behavior in the family or another group, returning in this way a sense of his neglect by others, is also showing his moral fiber. The learning here is often intermingled with reactions—and a reaction is of the same nature as the action.

An environment that does not show concern for the reality of the here-and-now life of a baby provides an education, or miseducation, in the field of ethics for that baby. For in judging and condemning others, one meets the possibility of a judging capacity in oneself.

In the case of uncaring environments, a baby's reactions can form the basis of a social ethics where an eye is demanded for an eye, no forgiveness is shown, and love and charity have no place in considering other people's actions.

But because the self can move out of its involvements, get into other involvements, can notice and entertain other impacts, not all ways of responding are reactions.

The baby who considers the unpredictability of others may develop the attitude of "I would like to know" and deliberately enter into experiments to satisfy himself. He may tease, provoke, refuse, reject, change his mind at precise moments, decide to move from one attitude to another, and watch the impacts of all these movements on others. He may also watch how others relate and use his direct experience, and through his observations learn by proxy: how his parents fight or quarrel, how his brothers and sisters assert themselves and call in others for the decisions that end crises. He not only can see in these examples the behaviors that are available to him, in addition to those that come spontaneously, but also can see by his feelings and sensitivities that there are concomitant movements of the self. They may show him what siding with one party in a conflict can be, whether it is always the same in any circumstance, whether it is caused by fear, love, admiration, or other feelings, and can slowly turn it either into loyalty to one party or into compassion or into hatred. All these are moral attitudes and involvements. The self can use its intelligence to illumine these movements and associate cognitive, intellectual perceptions to the moral movements.

Activities that engage a child can force his alertness to the possession of property or to the ease with which he can grab other people's property. If an object is vital for an experiment, its presence will be required by the child, and he will know at once that its removal is injurious and will respond accordingly. Attachment to objects may be generated by this connection to them. But it is as easy for a child to know that he is being guided in his attempt to appropriate to himself what was not given him by his mood, his caprice, his engagement in an experiment designed to discover someone else's responses. If he finds greed in himself and indulges it and is allowed by others to indulge in it, then greed will become a motive for some of his actions in relation to others. If his greed is checked by other people's greed or by calls to reason, he will develop a more shaded view of the social dynamics in his environment. If his greed prompts him to trick someone and surreptitiously take away what he knows to have been in someone else's hands, he may have an opportunity to judge whether he has accomplices in his milieu—or he may be told to return the object.

## Experience and the Moral Sense

No doubt there are many opportunities every day to make moral judgments. But they do not always occur in the field of property, nor do they comprise a systematic approach to morality. Years of experience may produce only disjoint samples which do not fall within one category, easily perceived and labeled. Contradictions may be let in and maintained again and again, which indicates that moral judgments are not intellectual judgments with a simplistic logic superimposed on them. Love, for instance, generates forgiveness, and forgiveness eliminates the attaching of a single positive or negative sign to each behavior. Forgiveness itself is not a rigid movement; sometimes it is brought in, sometimes it does not show itself, and the reasons why may be inaccessible. Hence the part played by the intellect in the field of ethics is as another variable added to judgments; it is not an organizer of judgments, as logic is. In the field of ethics circumstances count and alter conclusions radically. It is a new adventure for the self to learn in the moral field, and one life may not be sufficient to sort everything out.

Another area of ethical experience surrounds the notion of equitability. Is one treated like others or differently? Is one given as much of what one likes as are others? Who is given more? Who can be given less without arousing a feeling of sympathy?

To know equitability at this level, one needs only to own perception. It then becomes obvious if one has not been given a share comparable to the share that others get. But even perception may not trigger indignation, the companion of the sense of fairness. For example, a small child does not protest if he sees his father being served a larger share of food. Perhaps the child believes that fairness is being observed because he notices the difference between his size and his father's.

To develop the content of equitability requires an awareness of many concomitant facets. The study of cheating, by oneself and others, is one such area—for example, how one accepts one's own cheating and covers it up, finding excuses or invoking reasons that may convince or puzzle other people. This study, undertaken in various circumstances, may lead to the acceptance or the abhorrence, of not being oneself in a number of circumstances, of hypocrisy.

The moral sense, associated with the sense of truth, may find that when one's actions meet with disapproval in oneself and move one to seek the forgiveness of the injured person, what one is going though has attributes that require the label of regret or sorrow. To be sorry and long for pardon is always easier when one sees at once the injuries caused by one's actions. One also learns to be sorry for others who suffer, even if one has not oneself caused the suffering, as when we see someone fall or hurt in an accident. Sorrow is "being sorry" magnified, and belongs to the universe of morality.

But one can also learn to reduce the spectrum of sympathy and compassion, to become touched only by certain circumstances and by impacts beyond a very high threshold. One then changes oneself into someone who displays indifference, callousness, cruelty. It is even possible to learn to operate selectively, sharing compassion in some cases and showing cruelty in others. The co-existence of such contradictory moral attitudes in one mind makes moral judgments subject to a more subtle kind of consistency than true or false logic and proves both the flexibility of the mind and the complexity of living in the world at large where truth, moral truth, is harder to define than it is in the areas of the exact sciences.

A loving and caring father may, in his role as a statesman, refuse to forgive someone else's son for having been as moral as he could be in, say, following his conscience and refusing to go to war. An honest man may see no wrong in eating to ease his hunger while he does nothing to relieve the hunger of his neighbors. A businessman may see no wrong in a deal that promises what he has no certainty of delivering.

## The Sense of Truth and the Moral Sense

The logic of life is a suspended logic, sometimes applied and working, sometimes needing to be re-opened to let in factors that alter the results of mechanical logic.

The moral sense within the individual knows that the presence of unknown facts, views, possibilities does not allow one to reach a fixed conclusion, and is prepared to recast its position when a new factor is brought in. Instead of sticking to the premise and using a rigid method—a logic given in advance—the moral sense functions within the perpetual re-opening of the premise or even its replacement, so that another view can prevail. The logic of ethics functions like that of the intellect so long as there is no need to let in new factors; but when a new light illumines the facts of life, mechanical logic retreats and is no longer compelling.

Sometimes the boundaries of retreat are met, and then one speaks of a "matter of principle"—that is, the premises that coincide with the functioning of the individual's moral sense in harmony with the sense of truth as it has constituted one's personality from all experiencing.

It is the sense of truth that provides the logic of the moral sense. Because we recognize that we live in ignorance, we yield to the appearance in our consciousness of what we had ignored and change our stand and position. Truth illumines the moral sense, and the will mobilizes the content of the self to make the self adopt a new attitude. The new attitude is as revisable as the previous one, provided the revised attitude agrees as did its predecessor, with our experience.

## Conscience and the Moral Sense

Conscience is consciousness at work in the realm of ethics and is therefore the form in which the self asserts its presence in that realm.

Conscience, as a distinct component of the self, becomes aware of itself much later than do the functionings that trigger indignation, compassion, remorse, guilt, a need to be forgiven, to forgive, to widen oneself to make room for heretofore unacceptable behaviors (of oneself or of others), to cope with sorrow while expressing grief.

To know ethics at work, to know one's conscience, requires the unpredictable circumstances that can affect one because one simply is immersed in life; it is unlikely, therefore, that anyone can develop a system as organized as a science to cope with ethical events.

But individuals can form a system, like a rigid functioning, that occupies the mind and controls the brain so that some moral perception will trigger definite responses, in a manner similar to those biological behaviors in which reflexes take care of ordinary challenges. Such systems at work in individuals can be further systematized as collective moral behaviors. These in turn affect newcomers to a society and generate the conviction that such reflex functionings are "natural," the only possible choice for facing certain happenings.

When such community-wide systems exist, they are accompanied by the belief that the moral self has been molded from outside—God-ordained, or socially ordained, or as an expression of economic survival disguised as a principle handed down through the generations, and so on. Collecting such systems is the job of anthropologists. These workers give to values as objective a reality as actions and find how the values mold collective and individual behaviors. Orthodoxy is the label for a way of living that is molded by traditional values. Since traditional values have to be learned as a system, they involve the formation in the brain of sets of reactions to subtle social perceptions. Children have to spend years in acquiring the values and the reactions.

The concentration on established values has made available to people the time to be in contact with other aspects of life and therefore to become aware of other realms, but it has also made many people lose contact with their dynamic selves. It has made conscience a more primitive functioning of the self than consciousness. In the Romance languages, there is only one label for both phenomena, establishing an ambiguity that hides the dynamic component in the study of the self. A whole religion, Judaism, has been developed over many generations out of the conscious examination of conscience, and can serve students of ethics by supplying numerous examples of how man can color all living through the spiritual choice of what will make him man. Judaism embodies man's stories of consciousness knowing itself mainly as conscience, and of life knowing itself mainly as moral living.

All the other religions have offered moral codes, a number of them adopting the Judaic code. Hinduism, as one of the major world religions, leaves conscience suspended in consciousness, making self awareness the guide for ethics and truth a basis for morality.

## The Moral Realm

Who can doubt that one person has much to learn in becoming a moral being? Who can doubt that because of the entanglements of the many components of the self with the here-and-now, the realm of morality will be complex, challenging, capable of generating confusion, conflict, disease, alienation of a self no longer able to know itself and its functionings.

Because we grow in many realms at the same time, we can find in different layers of our organized, objectified selves, the mutual impacts of various awarenesses. Since these impacts are shot through with randomness because of the unpredictability of the environment, they cannot develop (as the soma or the brain integrate the past into the present opening towards the future) into a tidy organization in which the self links to the moral realm.

The self relates to the moral realm differently from the way that it links to the vital realm. Deep down in its contact with the vital realm are (1) equitability—all parts of the soma are equally in the care of the self; (2) accountability—the self knows it has the responsibility of maintaining all functionings at work, smoothly, and cannot delegate this responsibility to anyone else; (3) a reliance on itself to integrate what comes; and (4) a pretty good notion of what is happening—which is equivalent to a proper self esteem.

In the realm of the vital, the individual changes in order to cope with changes in the environment. In the realm of ethics the self also bends and changes appearances to survive, but the required changes can be re-examined and countered later if the self judged it necessary. Conversion is possible. The abandonment of symbolisms is possible. The extinguishing of remorse, guilt, and its replacement by total acceptance of the banned, the taboo, as a source of life, is possible.

One way to touch the moral sense is through an implied meaning, as in a parable where the literal meaning is the wrong meaning and the hidden, implied, meaning reaches the self through a complex alchemy.

If the moral sense has been misled because one has been manipulated by the environment, it is open to the self, when it find this out, to stress through rebellion a deeper functioning of the self in the moral realm. Every adolescent discovers this by himself, even if he loses it again because he lacks support from someone he admires. But the deeper functioning of the self in the moral realm can become a light to guide one's life if some inspiration is provided to counter the weight of tradition, the pressure from the community.

However inarticulate a child or an adolescent is in the field of ethics, what he feels is very real. His sense of truth provides the inner evidence, while the self provides both the necessary energy for indignation and the passion for asserting the moral stand. The will that sustains the expression of one's moral stand against someone else is nourished by the sense of truth. If the effort fails, the individual may find consolation in his rationalizations that the environment is too powerful and that one must compromise to survive. Examples of both rationalizations are found around us, and it is not always possible to decide through intellectual instruments who is right. In fact, moral issues can rarely find their reality in the abstract handlings of the intellect, and when it is asserted that the moral sense develops in parallel with the intellect, then contact with the concrete moral sense has in fact been lost and has been replaced by an awareness that focuses on verbalizing the rules of conduct—an intellectual activity. Social ethics may seem inescapable to those who yield to them. If such people happen to be students of the field of ethics, no wonder they come upon a yielding self and the ways it has adjusted to pressures rather than the actual variety of human experience.

Spinoza and Kant contributed greatly to the rational study of morality and ethics; they articulated for all of us the connection between the intellectual self and the moral self. Durkheim removed the moral sense from the individual and placed it in society, which alone, to his way of thinking, can know what young children obviously cannot know in this field. He gave to community education the job of molding a moral sense—which, thus, is no longer a gift, only a set of acquired behaviors that go with the awareness that society knows better than the individual and must be obeyed.

Some students of the brain have found there the seat of some behaviors that are associated with the moral sense, and have concluded that moral codes are carried by functionings of the brain as well as by society. They argue that a socially acceptable set of behaviors can be engineered by affecting those parts of the brain, which would lead individuals "to will" only what is "good" for them.

Now, since the self belongs to the four realms, it is always possible to find an equivalent to any manifestation of any component of the self in one realm in each of the other realms. The moral self can suffer from a traumatism experienced by any other sense or functioning; conversely, aggressions on the moral self can show symptoms at all levels, which can be made visible by the self or some instrument connected to the self. Damage to the brain can affect all senses, including the moral sense; accidents, drugs, electric shocks can provoke alterations in the basis of one's awareness and produce deviations of the moral sense; persistent societal pressures can distort views of the world, and the self can live in a damaged world, the only world it knows, where indignation is only aroused when its personal interest is touched. The moral sense still functions, but the self is no longer the arbiter, and awareness no longer attempts to know the actions of the self in relation to all others; there is only a restricted here-and-now with no tomorrow.

If the moral sense shows the power to encompass more and more of the moral universe, if it is associated with all the other expressions of the self, the self knows that to live a moral life is to live free—or rather, freedom is the expression of a self that is living and is taking itself into account into all the four realms, as well as everyone else in their four realms.

There is no boundary to morality because the self, through freedom and love, can produce more of the possible moral universe. This is the reason that society's morality shifts, and the moves that would have scandalized almost all past generations are taken for granted by the new generation.

Freedom is possible even in a world full of constraints because, at the human level, the self constructs everything and can transcend all its objectifications (somatic, behavioral, institutional) and find the creator of the world in itself. The creator of a new human reality.

Contact with this power of the self not only generates new possibilities of living by affecting the environment and extending behaviors and the uses of the soma and its functionings, but also shows that someone can take upon himself the eradication of prejudices and open the world to a deeper perception of its moral essence.

Morality does not evolve by adding something to it self. Just as a new instinct, by giving itself form, can produce a new animal species with space to express itself in the world, a new awareness of the self can give one man the opportunity to create a new world, first in the realm of ethics and later, when other men come to share his perception of values, in the realm of institutions.

If we describe as "pre-human" the men and women who have lost contact with the totality of themselves and instead of creating their universe to live in as they made their soma, believe that they live in a given, imposed universe, we can say that our world today is mainly formed of pre-humans. Instead of transcending the three basic realms to generate part of the fourth, they live in expectation that the immanent they pursue and intuit will take care of their needs and conduct. Pre-human morality exists as much as pre-human science, pre-human society, pre-human religion, etc. The character of all these phenomena stems from the pre-human characteristic of ignoring the power to transcend and thereby making the immanent actual and the transcendental available.

Reaching the Human stage means that a human being has found in his self all the entries to all his aspects and, in particular, recognized his own part in their functionings and in the creation of the many universes that become objective through his living them. To each of these universes he associates every one of his aspects.

We can all find around us all sorts of specimens of being, all equally viable, each representing one modality of being, each creating his society, his morality, his space for living.

If all this can be excreted or secreted by the cells in the brain, I would like to know how.

# 13 The Imaginative Self

If man has altered his habitat—to the point of threatening extinction for himself and all living creatures—it is due to a property of his self we call imagination.

Imagination, in the form of man using all his gifts and in the form of imagery closely related to some functionings of the brain, will serve to show that we have no other option than to adopt a perspective of man in which the mind and not the brain is the fast-evolving part.

## Making the Potential Actual

In our study so far, it was possible for us to show that in most learnings either the brain was directly educated to act as a synthesizer, an integrator of experiences, to free the self for subsequent tasks, or the brain's functionings were extended to generate new functionings of the self that barely needed to be linked to the brain to perform their duties or conquer new worlds.

## III
### The Mind Always Educates the Brain

When we recognize that the free energy of the self in sleep can be directed to the sense organs to be structured by them—producing dreams—we have discovered a new freedom for the self. Dreams are indeed examples of what can be done when imaging (or the process of making images) merges with symbolizing and intellectual activities. They not only do their jobs, these dreams; they also give the self an opportunity to know itself as the creator of what was not—as essentially a creator. When this power is taken from sleep and brought to the waking state and worked on by the consciousness of the waking state, it becomes imagination, everybody's birthright.

Side by side in the self live (1) an organizer of the content of the brain and the mind, which produces functionings compatible with all that is already present, and (2) an organizer of links between elements that are mutually exclusive at one level now made compatible at some other. This second organizer—more properly speaking, a functioning—is the expression of imagination.

To illustrate this functioning, the following examples will suffice. In mathematics, the intellect can formalize subtraction and keep the difference between two numbers in contact with three sets of objects: the set started with, the one taken away, and the one left over. The intellect actualizes in formal writing all subtractions that can be worked out in this way. Other subtractions are said to be "impossible"—for example, those in which the set taken away is "larger" than the set from which it is taken away. The role of the mind is to make the impossible possible. In this case, it does so by inventing negative numbers and accepting an answer which makes sense only within the new convention. If the mind is the place for such functioning, imagination becomes a function of the self.

Again in mathematics: the experience of counting sequentially carries with itself the experience of the practical impossibility of going on indefinitely. Eternity would be needed for the act. A movement of the imagination gives us a solution. The imagination says that we can make the potential actual, and this endows the mind with the results of "owning" infinity.

Indeed, to actualize the potential not only makes mathematics possible by making infinity available, it opens the gates to a number of other universes of which literature is not the least.

## The Transforming Mind

All kinds of engineering, all forms of technology, begin with an act of the mind that transforms the given, producing what is compatible with it but serving a new function. A stone becomes a hammer, another a knife or a blade, another a projectile, and so on.

In our crib, when we become aware that we can place our thumb against each of our fingers, this potential is transformed into a clasp, which in turn is transformed into a hook to permit us to sit up and later to stand up.

Awareness of transformation is a component of the working of the imagination, and it is needed in all the manifestations of the imagination.

As babies we soon discover that recognition is possible because we can complete the evocation of a fraction of the perception of anything and can trigger a trail of images made from different senses associated with this perception. We cannot fail to notice that associations are many and diverse and that the content of our consciousness is made of images, perceptions, feelings, impacts from the outside, and also a presence of our self in all. Nor can we fail to observe that this stuff is labile and held together from moment to moment by subtle links that can consist of any of the elements on which the self particularly dwells for its own reasons.

A crying child can be made to feel happy by a suggestion that evokes in him the idea of a new activity into which he can throw himself. At once his imagination is mobilized, and the invitation is accepted as the opening of an opportunity. The power to see beyond the present moment, to let the future get hold of the arena where one is, coupled with the working of re-cognition (which leads to the adoption of symbols), gives every child his entry into the world of the imagination, which is as real, in terms of awareness, as any other world, though different in a number of ways.

A perception gains meaning for a baby (or anyone) only if he supplies the material that transforms the percept into what caused its generator to produce it. For example, a movement of a hand in the air can be interpreted as putting a spoon into a bowl of soup and then handing it to someone to swallow; a rhythmical noise made by the tongue as the approach of a galloping horse on a cobblestone road; a posture as a duelist ready to use his sword; and so on. With interpretation, the reality at both ends of the communication can come to correspond closely. Yet the "transform," or what is in between, may be as insignificant and as unrelated to the content of the perception as a switch on a wall is to the light that fills the hall and illuminates everything.

As babies we acquire the facility of supplying some of our substance to complete the classes of impressions that go to form the "individuals" we need to be able to evoke. We have already mentioned the evocation of our mother who is familiar to us and is "allowed" to appear on our horizon as a smell or many smells, a texture or several textures, a voice, or any number of visual images. Our capacity for evocation can trigger any of the elements in the class, which allows us to have available the richness of the class. Although we all have the capacity to retain classes and to evoke any of the representatives they contain and feel the presence of the other elements in the class, we stress the "transform" associated with any of the elements so that we give ourselves the freedom of not specifying any of the elements and remain in contact with the richness. And we do this very early in life by becoming aware of the importance of transformation in all our knowing.

Without transformation there can only be crowding of the mind and paralysis of action. With transformation and the awareness that something in oneself is connected with the capacity to form a class of related impressions, we can use the storage capacity of the brain and be unencumbered by all the details.

Since the awareness of a world in change, in flux, is the true perception of reality by every baby, there is no miracle in the association of triggers with classes of impressions. The "transform" is the additional awareness of the simultaneous presence of triggers and classes, resulting in the freedom to focus on one or the other and to evoke both.

In the complex of the mind there is room for more than a number of these functionings that associate triggers and classes. The fertility of the imagination is found in the facility to hold in the mind a number of "transforms" and to engage in a game of transformation between them, among them.

If one is contemplating writing a story, the "transforms" are made along the axis of time, and the successive evocations are concatenated to produce a desired effect. The writer knows that all that he has written so far—which can trigger a sequence of evocations, which together trigger a climate, which in turn triggers expectations—must be related to what he wants to achieve and that he can legitimately engage only in a restricted number of transforms or else he produces chaos. A good writer is one who knows how to avoid chaos, to produce the unexpected that is nevertheless compatible with the climate and expectations, who knows how to show the power of the imagination or, as its equivalent, the variety of human experience.

## Imagination's Material

Imagination as a power of the self is available for all the manifestations of the self. But since the process of becoming acquainted with the actual possibilities of life takes time, and the means of entry into new universes form temporal hierarchies (necessary chronological sequences), our imagination, in its actual effect upon our life, appears differently at different moments. Its expression at those different moments makes it possible to describe imagination and to know it as an unfolding endowment of the self.

The application and education of imagination need some substance to work on, but since the substance can be formed of perceptions, feelings, images, relationships, memories, circumstances, conditions, situations, syntheses, vistas, visions, and soon, there is no end to what is possible to a self aware of the world it lives in and of its transformations. The role of the imagination is to actualize an awareness compatible with the dynamics of being in all the universes that the self can give itself.

Hence we find the need for imagination in economics as well as in painting, in administration as well as in composing music, in strategic studies as well as in dancing, in sociology as well as psychology.

Imagination can become fantasy, but it can also remain in contact with any other actual manifestation of the self. In fantasy it knows how much it can add to the riches of man; in actual manifestations it knows how much the self has penetrated the contemplated reality through the "transforms" compatible with it.

Jules Verne's imagination reached the present confines of space travel before the technology existed. He was fantasizing in the realm of the possible.

Hans Christian Andersen's imagination took him to the minute movements of awareness and made him create settings that magnified such movements, to force awareness in those who might miss noticing their importance while living in the world of relationship. His stories realize the "transforms" that enhance awareness.

Dostoevsky's imagination gives us a fantastic world of people doing to themselves and to others what could happen only through the movement of unrestricted impulses. The "transforms" he uses magnify some components of living, ignoring most others, and confront us with a world in which incarnate blind forces meet each other. Characters who are moved by passions that affect their perception of reality are accumulated to the point that the fiction seems to force the awareness of man-in-the-world as the maker of the world—the maker of as many worlds as there are men, as there are passions.

The imagination in every writer provides an entry to what is not oneself but could be. The reality of the characters filling the books of stories and the worlds they occupy comes from the world of imagination which, in a few verbal sketches, selects a few observations that makes them into the "transforms" that will trigger sufficient associations in the reader to evoke the impacts of real persons. The richer the evocation produced by the sketches, the deeper is the characterization.

When an artist disciplines his imagination, he does not impoverish it. Rather, he associates the functions of the imagination with a discrimination of what is essential and indispensable, and he uses this new functioning to guide the pen on the paper, the paint on the canvas, etc.

It is not easier or harder to associate disciplined imagination with fantasy or actuality. The proper "transform" must be found for both. Indeed, without actuality, finding the transform is as difficult as putting the concreteness of an apple into words.

## Using and Educating our Imagination

Everyday life provides many opportunities for educating our imagination. Re-cognition and symbolization are part of the functioning of the imagination; so is the acceptance of verbal statements as depictions of actions and feelings; so is the process of stressing and ignoring.

The sense of truth connects with the imagination in a dual relation: it supplies the component of what seems possible, grounded in reality, and it checks for compatibility as a form of the possible. The "ugly duckling," the "emperor's clothes" are illustrations of how appearances, although differing from reality, connect with reality via the movements of the mind. Our sense of truth, suspended for a moment when we receive the terms of reference of a story, comes in when we find that indeed things would be as the writer tells them if we accept the same terms. This experience shows the logic of fantasy broadening the functioning of the sense of truth.

Each of us who has day-dreamed of receiving showers of gifts and then engaged in how we would use and distribute them, has used many components of the self and been educated in the process. What would I be and what would I do if I had wings and could fly? If I were given the power to order everyone to do what I wish? If I were rich? If I were very intelligent? Or, at the other end of the spectrum, if I were abandoned by all my relatives and friends? If I were ill for a long time? If I could not be loved? And so on. Clearly, the imagination can supply a future for the present, and this alone makes it a special aspect of the self. This future, being possible, does not need to be actualized, or even to be probable, for the self to entertain it and find it valuable in its education.

Other functionings of the imagination need to be mentioned. One of them, associated with all experiencing, allows a sense of humor to function, humility to be present, readiness to see mistakes and errors and how to cope with them.

Another is to maintain in the self a sense that if one has entered into a situation, one can also come out of it, perhaps having learned some lessons, but mainly knowing that an entry and an exit go together. Often people who have not given themselves this education distinguish the in from the out and make one desirable, deliberate, and the other calamitous, accidental.

A third functioning of the imagination is the acceptance that whatever happens to others can happen to oneself. With this education we find a proper place in the universe, and we eliminate the illusion that somehow we are specially protected from pain, deception, hardships, abuses, and all those ills that befall our neighbors.

Another functioning of the imagination consists in looking at the solution to any problem as a beginning of many other problems and rejoicing in the happening because it states again that life goes on and that challenges are aplenty. If one's imagination does not supply this awareness, sometimes the blows of life do. The advantage of letting one's imagination function is that then the blows are not felt as blows but as part of the solution to the problem.

Another functioning of the imagination creates settings for the mind so that one can look at life from a certain distance, and restore saner proportions to the events in which one is involved.

Another is the ability to consider simultaneously a multitude of tracks, either keeping them separate (as when a chess champion defies scores of adversaries) or examining the relative merits of each track in a new design.

Another is not identifying "I do not know it" with "It does not exist" nor identifying "I cannot do it" with "It cannot be done"—

and similar "equations," all of which one would associate with stupid people if they had not often been maintained by learned men.

Another is to be struck by the familiar. This seems to be one of the rarest functionings. Yet it occurs commonly enough to fill the annals of human history and the history of science. To treat the familiar as unknown seems the opposite of what common sense would suggest, but it is a power of the imagination to give us this perception. Archimedes took a bath and shouted "Eureka!" Floating in the bath helped him to solve the problem of the composition of gold alloys. Jeremias Richter could not believe that two neutral solutions would remain neutral when mixed, although common sense suggested this to all the chemists of his time. His question and his answer made quantitative chemical analysis a possibility, even a necessity. Julius Robert Mayer, like all ship physicians, knew that the blood of the sailors he bled changed color in the tropics, but he asked himself why, and he was able to establish the first principle of thermodynamics, a cornerstone of the study of energy and modern technology.

Imagination is as much the guide of the scientist as of the artist because it is present as a functioning of the self in all living and is not the outcome of a special education.

That imagination can be educated and works differently in the various involvements of the self in actual living is another matter. The content of the images used by the imagination may condition the kind of exercises that are most valuable for some apprenticeship. But imagination gains its greater capacities when the self makes awareness of its actions the center of attention. By making imagination freer, by making it more vulnerable to more inconspicuous dynamics, we educate it for greater tasks.

If we become aware in the waking state that in sleep we have at our disposal a more compact universe—a universe in which the self commands and what happens can all be willed; a universe that is freer because the aggressions of those we cannot control are no longer actual; a universe in which energy is the actual content with which the self is in contact, making it possible to link anything to anything—we also become aware that imagination uses many functionings of the self and serves them as well. Artists, writers, scientists must all use more than their imagination to produce the objectifications in their lives, but they especially value their imagination as the stamp of their uniqueness, their personality, their contribution to their culture or to humanity.

By letting people know that imagination, although a variable from individual to individual, is the birthright of everyone and that it can be educated through exercises corresponding to the various functionings outlined above, we shall remove the prejudice that only the few, the "chosen," have been endowed with it. If we refuse to equate the works of the imagination solely with the socially valuable works of the imagination, we shall help everyone acknowledge that its functioning is not tied to particular results.

The results of the imagination may or may not have the additional properties that make them valuable to others. In fact, true works of the imagination are not always immediately recognized by the public as specially valuable to society. The Impressionists may serve as an example.

Imagination as a property of the self can play a part in making it possible for Human Education to replace the obsolete educations still practiced in our world; in this new education, the awareness of imagination's contribution to all endeavors will explode the artificial boundaries imposed upon minds when they are treated as independent of the self. Imagination is needed to recognize boundaries and their artificiality, and to remove them through invented exercises that bring to the center of awareness what needs to be done.

# 14 The Aesthetic Self

If there is an area where the self clearly transcends the brain in its total functioning, and must therefore be considered as the prime mover, it is the field of aesthetics.

Here we will examine aesthetics through different frames of reference.

## The Changing Forms of Beauty

However confidently each of us can state that some experience is beautiful, the perception of beauty is an acquired response, and not all of us agree about it in the way we can agree about pain or brilliance or noise.

The history of art is there to teach us that painters formed schools, that new schools did not find it easy to be accepted by the establishment, and that the new schools could take their place only when the old schools disappeared and a sufficient number of fans supported the new—to become in turn the entrenched establishment. It seems that taste is as much a cultural as an individual product.

Whatever is perceived beyond the perception of objects, colors, design, which leads to the statement that something is beautiful, is the result of education. How many musicians of one culture find themselves completely lost when confronted with the "strange" music of another culture? How many adults in one culture find the sounds that thrill their children atrocious?

In Western culture alone, we find many instances of new sensitivities that then become the common taste. Few people can believe that to perceive the beauty of glaciers, brooks, trees, clouds, etc., we needed the education that Rousseau and the Romantics provided for their generations. But literature is there to provide a witness—first, to the absence of openness to the beauty of nature and then, suddenly, to an almost universal interest in it. Similarly with paintings, which just as suddenly become dedicated mainly to nature in a thousand different forms.

During the present century, the concept of beauty came to be stretched to the point that cubism, Dadaism, and many other isms, pop art and pop music, could all claim title to being labeled beautiful.

## What is Beauty?

If one's self cannot deny the realm of aesthetics to itself, if beauty is an attribute of reality, how does the self know beauty?

Bergson suggested that lines command our sight to follow them and that beauty is experienced by the ease of surrender to the lines. The self can know whether it is made to yield or is stopped in its movement, jolted, woken up by the unexpected, the irregular, the jeering—and can experience the awareness that the brain is not soothed, does not dissolve into what it contemplates. But this awareness cannot be accepted as one of beauty, of aesthetics. Bergson's suggestion seems not to meet the problem.

If it were habits that commanded our tastes, then of course the sense of beauty would belong to the brain and only the content of what moves us would be cultural. All men, having brains, would be impressed by beauty and would relate to aesthetics as they do to sex, to different kinds of food, more through temperament and appetites than through a consideration of the contemplated thing itself.

But such a state of affairs does not describe the universe of aesthetics that seems superimposed on all other worlds.

The sense of beauty seems to have several sources.

Beauty is experienced as a concomitant of the functional. When something seems to respond best to the conditions that regulate the existence of an edifice, a road, an expanse of water, a vehicle, etc., the perception of it simultaneously carries the assessment of functionality and beauty. The satisfaction experienced in the perception ensures its acceptance as functional and causes the self to testify to the presence of an aesthetic feeling.

Sometimes the feeling arises from the appearance of an opening into that which does not seem to belong to the experience in which one is involved. Such an experience generates the feeling that besides the perceptible, behind the obvious, a mystery is operating and it mobilizes the self.

There are a few theorems in mathematics that clearly contain, besides a mathematical content, a breadth that uplifts mathematicians, that leaves them in a state which can only be called spiritual and that may be expressed with the exclamation, "Beautiful!" One, for instance, is the very old theorem of Euclid, that the sequence of prime numbers is infinite; another is the less-than-100-years-old theorem of Cantor, that the scale of infinities is transfinite.

The aesthetic experience here results from the awareness that infinity is present, tangible, passing from the intellect to the whole self acknowledging itself as a witness to a precise event, chiseled in its simplicity but unlimited in its promise. Cantor's theorem, in particular, takes one's breath away while giving life to a whirl of thoughts that seems to have a beginning but can never end. As if the aesthetic experience resulted from the self leaving behind the anchor of the brain and all it stands for.

## The Awareness of Beauty

Clearly this kind of inebriation is not maintained by the continual additional of exciting material; it is self-perpetuating, it becomes a sensitivity vulnerable again and again to an evocation or a perception. That is why the poet says, "Beauty is in the eye of the beholder." However many times one reads a poem that one finds beautiful, no fatigue sets in, and familiarity does not reduce its appeal. However many times two true lovers meet, they know each meeting as if it were the first. However many times one hears a great piece of music, the experience is renewed in depth, as if one felt the piece for the first time.

But when awareness leaves the scene, familiarity sets in, perception is dulled, even annihilated, and one does not seem to suspect the existence of a source that can touch one's sense of beauty. Outsiders, strangers, may be moved by something that belongs to others who do not value it, either because they do not perceive it or perceive something else in it. Glaciers have been in their place for millions of years, but mountain people have not always sung their beauty. Forests have every year changed their leaves in the fall, but the glory of the color symphonies has not always moved those who looked at them.

For the Romantics, it was the special presence of an exalting self in their perception that generated the opportunity to become aware of the qualities of the perception. Animating nature was a deliberate act of awareness, and it made available, from then on, both a low threshold of vulnerability and an amplifying sensitivity that recognized the presence of the self in the experience more and more.

Because the self can entertain such dialogues with any of its involvements, aesthetic experiences can be found in all walks of life, and the word "beautiful" fits a large spectrum of perceptions.

One can see an open-heart operation as beautiful—if one does not faint, if one has disciplined oneself to take care of the feelings of sympathy and compassion for the patient, if one has managed to become acquainted with the many technicalities, precisions, and organizations required, if one takes all this in one's stride and can let the functional gestures strike one through their sobriety, swiftness, economy, and obvious purposefulness. At this level of being, in which the self is simultaneously open and controlled, the selected vulnerability allows an awareness that one is perceiving both something that harmoniously takes care of the demands of the present and the spectacle that meets the eye.

On the whole, one can see beauty only after one has worked on oneself, although the self is vulnerable to the perception of smooth functionings from it s prenatal experience. The perception of beauty, as distinct from the perception of smooth functioning, makes aesthetics a vital experience but also a luxury. It is possible not to be aware of the many aesthetic manifestations around one simply by not cultivating vulnerability to those manifestations. In some fields only special experiences can prepare one for the reception of the impacts that will trigger a response that is recognizably aesthetic. Mathematics is not of universal appeal, though everyone who has paid the price in time and dedication can perceive its beauty. The merging of two corporations, which only a few people directly perform, can appeal aesthetically, if at all, only to those who know what it entails.

The bringing up of children, which covers day after day and extends over years, can be judged aesthetically by outsiders, but it also can be lived as a beautiful unfolding, extending over all the moments of all the days over all those years, beautiful in spite of the constant meeting of crises, of the demands of events and circumstances, because the self finds itself installed in the throbbing relationship, feeding back liveliness, alertness, compassion, understanding, fitting responses, and the resolution of tensions. The aesthetics of human relationships are for those who cultivate them, who give themselves to their actuality and not to an idea of what they should be.

The aesthetics of love-making for lovers is not identical with perceiving the beauty of two lovers lost in their embrace, which is for outsiders. In fact, even lovers who perceive each other do not necessarily perceive the beauty of their love-making; it must become the object of perception <u>per se</u> and be isolated from pleasure, from the satisfaction that all of the subsidiary components are working well. The aesthetics of love-making are known to the self that can reach beyond sensuality, sexuality, eroticism, the essence of being merged in the couple, to being oneself because of the other and making the other be because of oneself. The aesthetics of love-making are reached when the ego is transcended and replaced by an all-pervasive feeling that one can live forever in this state, not seeking release, not refusing to be as one is made to be in the couple. For the male to know that no orgasm is needed, for the female that orgasm is not an event but a state of being, not reached as a peak from which to drop, but a peak at which to stay, naturally, effortlessly, indefinitely.

The association of pleasure with aesthetics tells us only that the biological component has been satisfied. In man, even pain can become a source of aesthetic experience, known only to those who do not shirk it—and also do not pursue it to satisfy a secondary pleasure experienced in the mind or in one part of a split personality. Pleasure in the masochist or the sadist maintains a dysfunction of the self, and one can say that it is not concerned with aesthetic. Job's pain, on the contrary, with its paroxysms and its association with his total givenness to the study of righteousness in his life and the transcendental mercy of God for his servants, generates a strong aesthetic feeling in those who truly understand it. Pleasure and pain may in fact have nothing to do with the aesthetic self since man has been able to see beauty in many hidden corners of his self.

## The Thresholds of Aesthetic Feeling

There is perhaps a pair of individual thresholds for any feeling within which the self acknowledges a perception that goes to make the sensing of beauty. Perhaps a special sensitivity to these thresholds arouses by itself in each of us the immediate concomitant of aesthetic feelings, and also warns us when something has been violated in the field. If this were so, we could understand why, for example, the moods of lovers can suddenly change as soon as the behavior of one falls outside the spectrum of the accepted and acceptable.

As soon as the thresholds on either side are violated and allowed to occupy consciousness, as soon as the self acknowledges the thresholds, rather than all that which was concomitant with them, the new state, now so different from the previous one, expresses the mood of the self seeing itself in transition.

It may be that the very adherence of the self to the boundaries of the spectrum of aesthetic experiences makes the self peculiarly vulnerable to their violations and generates moodiness, in some cases extreme. "Tolerance" expresses the opposite of this adherence, even when the spectrum is just as narrow.

Lovers are guided in their gift of themselves by this alertness to the way their partner relates not only to them but to thresholds of acceptance. Musical audiences similarly relate to the execution of pieces with respect to the spectrum and its boundaries.

In fact, our common language recognizes "ugly" words with the same functioning (that of creating boundaries) as "beautiful" words. Social habits create the boundaries and the adherence to them, the capacity to be shocked, to blush, to feel attacked and hurt. Social etiquette produces similar possibilities.

Besides these functionings, met in most of us, there are some functionings that can be found only among those who give themselves to the aesthetic experience in a particular field and who seriously want to know whether they can extend it for themselves and incidentally for all.

The history of the arts can supply us with cases to study.

Sometimes we can find there an explorer who enters into a dialogue of his own and deliberately imposes on himself the production of a work that will prove to himself that the aesthetic experience has been expanded. Van Gogh and Cezanne have succeeded in such an effort, and suffered in doing so. Their paintings are not simply beautiful pictures, they are dialogues of the total self with the aesthetic self through a medium and a topic that permitted them to explore the tension. Mallarme, Rimbaud, and Verlaine used words for the same end and enriched French literature by extending aesthetic expression. Beethoven and Wagner, however differently, each exploded the boundaries of musical aesthetics by exploring complexity, but they remained accessible because they kept the previous spectrum as part of their own. The cultural shock in their contemporaries resulted from adherence to thresholds (more in some cases than in others) rather than from a refusal to accept the new, a response that, often legitimately, throws innovators back into obscurity.

Sometimes an idea takes hold of some artists who then collectively explore the extent to which it can remain compatible with the spectrum of sensitivity to beauty held by the members of their community, resulting in more tolerance to what is beautiful. The "naturalistic novel" of more than one hundred years ago, "pop art," "rock music," illustrate this point. They do not all necessarily produce works of art that can join the examples that educate the aesthetic sense in a culture, but some do, and they serve as frames of reference in the study of a culture's evolution of taste.

It seems that the taste that indicates to outsiders our sense of beauty (in all realms) can be educated to conform. But it is also true that our selves can affect taste and broaden it, first by making the self consider a new aesthetic problem and then by finding the way to become vulnerable to norms of aesthetics that were not formerly considered. The problem of entertaining Oriental or African music for Westerners, and vice versa, can serve as illustrations.

## Aesthetics and Perfection

Another movement of the self that provides a frame of reference in the field of aesthetics, is a feeling for perfection. Throwing a stone to skim the surface of a pond, producing a succession of contacts, starting sets of ripples, together produces satisfaction that goes far beyond the feeling associated with a functioning that is smooth and to the point. The impact of the event brings to the self a consciousness: "Perfect!" There is nothing more to ask for.

Whenever consciousness reaches this spontaneous conclusion, leaving the self fully satisfied and generating the respect that goes with full acceptance, the self experiences what we intellectually know as perfection.

Because our contact with perfection leaves us satisfied, we do not have to remember what we experience. But since we nevertheless do retain impacts from sources of perfection, we now have available two ways for the self to be lastingly touched. In one, we integrate the impacts by changing the self and its expression, no longer knowing how we related before in that area but knowing how we do now, perfection being our frame of reference. In the other way, we maintain a track in the brain for each of the experiences and its links, and we can totally trigger that content of the brain by using any item. Imagery accompanies the second approach but not necessarily the first. In both cases we can appreciate the aesthetics in a situation. In the first without needing comparison; in the second, most likely through checking the impact against evoked samples of what we call perfection.

\* \* \*

Like the self in all its other manifestations, the aesthetic self evolves, and tastes change. If we can maintain our contact with our aesthetic sensitivity, we not only receive beauty but produce beauty—and possibly do so in every one of our manifestations, making aesthetics a dimension of each moment of life. No doubt we can all conceive of this as a way of being for ourselves.

# 15 The Mystical Self

The self can be aware of all its functionings and activities—of its objectifications, of the free energy that takes the form of dynamics within and between the objectifications, of its vulnerability and sensitivities, of the kind of activity it is engaged in, whether it is operating at the level of affectivity or that of the intellect, whether it is asleep or awake. But it can also be aware of awareness, of knowing itself and how it relates with any part of life. It can also sometimes transcend all involvements, and while being entirely with itself, it can know the universe of being as such, the universe of the ineffable that is beyond expression.

Whenever the self knows this, it knows what transcends the knowledge of all other realms, it knows directly that it is part of the cosmos, of the same stuff, that it is one with the processes of creation.

Many of these moments, scattered through everyone's life, continuously for some, intermittently for others, have a quality that the self recognizes as the highest reality. It is the highest, whatever its origin and with whatever symbols it can be connected, simply because the self cannot do better than be entirely with itself, quietly leaving all its forms to the functions already generated, so as to "turn" all it is and all it has freely towards itself.

This state of the self—similar in appearance to the state of sleep, closed to the distractions of impacts, but this time from within as well as from without—can be known to itself as the wakened consciousness taken precisely to the "center" of the self. All the contradictions that follow from the fragmentary presence of the self in its experiences—of being awake and not at the disposal of outside impacts, of not being asleep although closed to impressions, of being totally given to something without content, empty and full at the same time because the space where the self is has no representation, completely alone but never so fully related, affirming the will by total surrender, seeing all and noticing nothing, knowing the eternity of a moment—disappear and have no impact, leaving the self whole, quiet, intense, unconcerned, sure that this state is the most human state available. If the self that knows itself in this way is called mystical, we can say that the fourth realm begins with this expression of the self.

## The Mystical Self in the Growing Child

As a baby, the opportunity to trigger the mystical return of the self to itself can occur as frequently as being placed at a certain hour in a certain position, exposed to an atmosphere warmed by sun, light, and sound, all integrated into cozy surroundings, the self balancing itself to blend all impacts and reduce their power of distraction. It can occur as frequently as being in the arms of the loving one who gives warmth and tenderness, makes no demand for anything other than being, and establishes a give-and-take that fuses two beings, thereby presenting the baby with an opportunity to extend himself while receiving a wonderful presence from someone else. As frequently as being in a bath supported by caring and tender hands so that the extension of the self, experienced as relaxation and confidence, blends with the integration of warmth and weightlessness provided by the water.

In the mother's womb, the unborn child possibly has opportunities for knowing itself in a mystical way and no doubt grasps them. For the movement of the self away from the objectification of the moment and away from knowing itself in its environment (inner and outer) may be required to allow the working of the future, to enable the unborn child to enter the intuition that will guide the making of oneself as a human soma. Can the future do its work without the mystical self? Since the past presses and conditions, where can the freedom of the self—which is linked with its future and can exist only through its future—find its rightful place if there is no mystical self available?

Since the mystical self manifests itself by an awareness that the self is in harmony with the universe, that the self has access to the totality of power in the cosmos, that it is whole with an open future, such awarenesses make the self an optimist who seems to know that goodwill is coming its way. "Good" may mean only what one wishes, and then it may not happen; but it also may mean the challenges that lead to growth, and life is full of them.

Boys and girls generally share this optimistic disposition, looking forward to every new day, for each one brings the opportunity to feel that the universe is expanding. In all the manifestations of the self at this time of childhood, action is the focus of attention, and it transforms the inner and outer environments. Since the activities lead to greater skills, and memory takes the form of functionings available to the self, the self knows the inner and outer worlds as one continuum and actually lives in the cosmos. The mystical self, although only superficially aware of the unique texture of the inner-outer world, does not abandon this awareness; it neither excuses it with metaphysics nor pretends that it does not exist. Symbolism is accepted as simply as facts are, and social and natural reality are barely distinguished.

This continuity of inner and outer will break down at adolescence, when the inner life is exalted and the outer life becomes a realm belonging to others. For a few years the yearning to perceive the unity of life will move the self to mobilize all that it is and has to resolve the duality that causes such painful awarenesses. In this period, the mystical self is enhanced, is nourished with all the passions that now flood the self, the sense of the new powers available to the self in its physical growth, its biological transformations, its new capacity to use an intellect bathed in affectivity. Mysticism gains a separate reality, becomes attractive to the self, promising the total union that love, intelligence, vulnerability to greatness, all make desirable. Mystics become sources of inspiration to adolescents, leading to actual or virtual (imagined) trials in the attempt to become like them. From such trials the self either finds the permanent presence of the awareness of the mystical self in all its does, or discovers that the ideal is too high and had better be foregone.

## The Mystical Self, the Brain, and the Senses

The men and women that adolescents will become may know the same choice as adolescents, or may opt for something in between that remains the compromise imposed by "realism."

Still, each of us has known that there is a mystical side to life, and as soon as a door opens and the light pours into the self, conversion takes place, a turning around of functionings that now brings within what before was left outside and dedicates the time of life to living the conversion.

The brain no doubt plays many roles in facilitating conversion. First, it releases energy that was bound to the images that maintained the climate within. Second, it allows a new dynamics to use the already available pictorial and verbal material that is in harmony with the feelings governed by the new awareness. This functioning, which is old but now seems to be new because of the way things are arranged, teaches the brain to replace certain dynamics rather than to erase the past and produce new impacts. Conversion tells us something about the way the brain can function.

Third, the brain, in so far as it cannot be removed from the path of feelings, finds the appropriate attributes that make it possible to adjust to the demands of mysticism. In the case of the baby in a cozy, warm environment, this attribute is an inhibition of imagery, so that what the baby already knows does not interfere with the gift of the self to the whole. In the case of older children who are not yet adolescent, who feel the promise of the adventures to come, the attribute is maintaining the size that fits the demands of action, hence, an inhibition on the growth hormones originating in the pituitary. In the case of the adolescent, the release of this inhibition as well as the enhancement of the resonance of the single impacts that give to each moment a deeper, more lasting echo, are the attributes akin to the brain's functionings. The adolescent's brain is used differently because of the chemical upheaval brought about by the releases of hormones. It is now possible for the self to know all the nuances of emotions as lasting impacts—first, because the brain is equipped for such studies, and second, because the adolescent gives himself to emotions, to their creation, their enhancement, their exacerbation.

At the peak of its stretching of each emotion, the self learns what it can stand. To maintain itself at that peak, that threshold, is the work of the mystical self, now engaged not in turning away from the soma but in extending itself over its somatic functionings.

No doubt the choice of one and the same language by mystics and lovers comes from the proximity of both to the same threshold, although on opposite sides. To have passed from one side to the other makes the relationship to the brain utterly different. In one, it is conceivable that chemicals from the outside can be integrated with the lovers' manifestations and become aphrodisiacs. In the other, the control of one's chemistry from a higher level makes additional chemicals superfluous, or rather allows them to be generated in the brain by the self, which is now turned towards being itself beyond its objectified form. Rather than taking chemicals, the ascetic mystic, through fasts and penances, through prolonged prayer and meditation, gives the brain the opportunity to generate the chemicals that will allow him to go on with his own use of his soma and his mind.

No mystic has known mysticism by quitting the soma. The spirit (equivalent to what we have all along called the self) does not manifest itself in the mystical act without a soma, although the stresses on the somatic functionings are indeed different. The spirit neither despises nor rejects the soma. It treats it as it can be treated, as sets of functions that are not directly energized by the presence of the self but still function, available for when the self returns to the realm of everyday life.

## The Mystical State

The mystics, whose symbolisms attribute their mystical states of being to a visitation from the supernatural and who view the termination of these states as an abandonment, know directly what it is to be on either side of the threshold that they cross when moving into the mystical state, and they lament the loss of the state when they return to their daily self. In the mystic states they know of a world that guarantees them that this life, their ordinary state of being in it, is not the whole of reality. The mystical self knows mysticism as the way of knowing the transcendental. Because the mystical self is the same self as the one that objectified the soma and the brain, it also knows what the transcendental is and how to expand the self to dwell in it. As soon as this has been done, the transcendental acquires a quality of immanence somewhere between the objectified and the transcendental. The self can now treat the immanent with all the instruments it has given itself, and can raise itself to integrate the immanent into its life. The descent of the future is, once more, visible to the self. Whether this descent needs to reach the level of a functioning of the brain depends on whether more of the brain can be produced to deal with such functionings or whether the mystic chooses to use the immanent for further transcendences.

St. John of the Cross, who lived his mystic self at three levels, knew how to put his visitations into a poem using his personal symbolism and how to put into current theological language the content of his poems. The writing of the poem required a certain descent into the uses of the mind, the brain, and the soma; the commentaries required an observance of the cultural and social circumstances of his time. This shows how the level of the mystical experience is four or five stages removed from the objectification of the soma.

## Paths to the Transcendental

The ordinary person who wants to transcend the manifestation of his ordinary self and give himself an entry into the states that are beyond the folklore of mankind can consider many proposals. Dervish dances, fasting, drugs, hypnotism, all begin with a self that is aware of the soma and through it the brain and that then force the self to detach its awareness from the soma and the brain to be available for what comes in the resulting states. In Western laboratories, biofeedback seems more convenient, more modern, and perhaps just as good. These approaches all tell us that the ordinary man has a hunch that he possesses all that is necessary to manifest his mystical self but still lacks the education that could have given him a knowledge of mysticism.

The paths to the transcendental are many and varied. Hassidism is a way of knowing the spirit in which conscience and a covenant with a personal God are never forgotten. Sufism is another way, in which the reality that is behind the forms of experience and that can unite mankind, is reached by shaking out the forms, by emptying the mind. Taoism too proposes reaching out to the void as the method for men to find Man. Zen Buddhism invites men to remove the shield that separates them from the transcendental through a sudden encounter, beyond the apparent orderliness of the world, with one's bafflement.

Tantra takes the route of purifying each of the forms of the objectified energy that dwells within people so as to eradicate any involvement. Schools of Hinduism offer various disciplines that ultimately aim to unite the self with the transcendental, maintaining that men need several lives to accomplish the whole climb unless, as in Christianity, a kind of grace produces the result overnight.

## III
### The Mind Always Educates the Brain

No philosophy—and still less a single sentence summary of it—can be equated with the actual living of the concrete movements of the self (which has endowed itself with a soma and its functionings, with a mind and its functionings, and with all that is beyond the soma and the mind but can be given by the self to itself, like intelligence, an intellect, sensitivities, memory) towards that which is not yet. We have singled out the mystical self as an aspect of the self distinct from all the others studied earlier in this book, because it serves the purpose of meeting ourselves as we are, having systematically managed to transcend conditions that go back to the beginning of the cosmos, the beginning of life, the beginning of the transformations of life that produce all the species there are, and the purpose of meeting ourselves as we go on managing transcendence in our individual lives.

To account for this power of transcending any of the conditions in which we place ourselves, the mystical aspect of the self seems a proper awareness. Since mankind has considered mysticism in all religions in all civilizations that have left behind expressions of themselves, we cannot say that we have invented an <u>ad hoc</u> explanation of man's manifestations; rather that we have been able to bring together in a functional synthesis the facts of everyday life and the facts of those given to transcending their universes who succeeded in bringing back their ways of knowing to us. We do not have to look at mystical experience as a peculiar state of consciousness. As a state of consciousness, yes; but one that is open to everyone as a self, provided he does what is required to get into it and stay in it. Just as he must meet the necessary requirements to produce works of art, works of science, works of artisanship, etc.

# 15 The Mystical Self

The self, so multifaceted, can know itself and use some of the forms of expression that it gave itself to let others know it. This applies to the mystical self as well.

# 16  The Evolving Self

This chapter will serve as a summary, as a depository of conclusions derived from the studies of the previous chapters, as the announcement of a beginning for some of us, as a balance sheet of what we have been able to do with what we have invested in our lives.

As soon as we put the self engaged in living consciously at the center of our human studies, there seems to be no end to what can be looked at, to the gains in significance, to what can come out of it for us as human beings.

At the present juncture, when we see chaos on the economic, social, political planes, when all philosophies, religions, beliefs, are doubted or are seen as devices for the exploitation of man by men or of men by a few men, when all kinds of evangelists with simplistic solutions to collective ills are hailed as saviors, when the hopes generated by technology and science meet head on with the fears of pollution and genocide, when the planet Earth has become a crowded space ship, full of misery, pain, crime, when each of us is made to feel the troubles of everyone of us almost at the moment that they happen, it may seem curious that our vision of man today can remain that of a fast-evolving being and still be true to the moment. Nothing that happens today is strange to those who have reached the awareness that awareness guides all our actions and our thoughts, our movements and our inertia.

It is no longer possible to belong to today and shift the responsibility to others. All idols have been pulled down. The rulers of the world are seen to be either ordinary men or usurpers. Man's destiny is in a few men's hands, who are perhaps insane, perhaps misled, perhaps misguided, perhaps wise. God may know what He (or She) wants for mankind, but mankind is in charge of handling His (or Her) orders. Man affects man all along, from conception to burial or cremation or disintegration. With this perception, all human failings have become part of the fabric of Earthian living. And all human possibilities too. And for the first time in man's history on Earth, anyone of us can alter the course of that history for evil or for good.

Evil is no longer defined as contrary to what should be, nor is good defined as the agreement with what should be in the eyes of the Establishments. Evil is what <u>will</u> ultimately stop the movement of mankind towards its clear destiny of leaving everyone free to give expression to himself functioning in harmony in the four realms, and good <u>is</u> all that which makes it easier.

Because of the complexity of each moment, no one can assess, in terms of good or evil, the value of any event, the death of anyone, a birth, a change of political regime, etc. Any demand for the <u>a priori</u> agreement of an event with a preconception thus must be considered evil, for the future remains unknown and to freeze it in a form of the past stops evolution.

Evolution here does not mean movement towards a pre-established end. It means only that all is in flux, all is a function of time, and that the next unknown stage will not be the last. Death is only philosophically the end of life (no doubt also medically and legally, but this does not influence the future). Evolution takes place in living people (and species), and each of us can only know himself as having grown. We are none of us born complete in every way. Each of us knows himself as changing, even if we do not always stress change as our obvious attribute. Those fundamentalists who philosophically reject "the theory of evolution" cannot factually deny growth in all places, including the moral plane. That is why they are aware of education and give it so much attention. Education would never exist if evolution did not. Even an education that only conditions.

Some people may want to hold the view that evolution was necessary until the redeemer came but that it is no longer needed since the path has been found and has been given us. Now we only have to change to be like Him. But that kind of change is not evolution. It may just be a grace dispensed by Him.

## III
### The Mind Always Educates the Brain

Evolution is not an acceptable description of man if it concentrates on the point at which man emerges from the third realm. But it is needed if we want to make sense of the content of our awareness of the universe.

That we are in time, no one denies. The rhythm of day and night, of the seasons, is not in dispute. That we take time to reach enough maturity to be born, to go to school, to get married, to become an elder in the community, no one denies. What is denied is our link with the content of zoology books. That man is an animal and, as such, fixed in his set of behaviors—although the action of the molding consists precisely in making everyone according to an ideal.

The evolving self is needed to make the cosmos a man's world, and from the start man has affected his world. Anthropologists link the appearance of Man to the appearance of tools and thus acknowledge that man's evolution can be traced to the history of his impact on the environment, although they also see man's evolution as the outcome of the impacts of the environment on him. It is a two-way movement. Therefore, we need a model of man that is capable of taking account of all impacts, and this we have attempted in this book.

The instruments of man are only the tools he makes. Before tools can be invented, man must be vulnerable to some aspects of reality. Hence man must be capable of sensing in himself what he perceives and finding in himself the resources to transform his awarenesses into actions that agree with the perception and the intention. History (with prehistory) can tell us how long the process of making a tool has taken in the case of concrete people in specific settings on our planet. The time it took may have been so long that no awareness of the maker was required; progress may have been very slow when the tools had to be integrated into the actions that absorbed most of men's energy because they were necessary for survival. When an accumulation of tools made the impacts visible within one lifetime, it became possible to examine evolution on a scale that yielded some of its structure and significance.

Instruments and tools are preshaped in the mind, and we must today consider that the intellect, intelligence, symbolism, language, and so on, are instruments of the self, for the self to shape lives. This is why works like <u>Brave New World</u>, <u>1984</u>, and many others, appeal to readers in our time. The exaggerations do not make things less real. A warning is an instrument for illumining actions and opening up a possible future.

Today only the blindest among us do not see that evolution is at work, and at work is every one of us. Do not see that what one of us can do with himself could be done by others. Although the impacts man makes on the environment start with one individual, we no longer identify intelligence with grace granted from above. We no longer consider man's problems as curses and punishments, only as symptoms of the level of our evolution confronting complex challenges. We no longer believe that improvements in our living, our living conditions, and the amount of spiritual leeway we give ourselves, come from anywhere other than our concerted actions and our concern for certain realities. We no longer beatifically expect that God, the

Church, the State, the Government, the Elite, will mobilize something unspecified to give us what we wish or desire.

Instead we know that <u>we</u> must provide, <u>we</u> must do the right things, <u>we</u> must rise to the challenges, <u>we</u> must exert ourselves, be more vigilant, more industrious, more patient, more frugal, more courageous, more dedicated, much more intelligent, much more sensitive, much more imaginative, better educated on all planes to cope with a life that has increased its density through speeded-up impacts from television, the computer, rocketry. Intense living, even outside the hustle and bustle of city life, is with all of us, simply because we know much more about our endowments and have focused on our rights as persons of a particular age, place, status. Even solitude, the so-called empty life of autistic people, the silence of the deaf, the restricted world of the retarded, are dense and become more fully furnished every day as more sensitive people look at them. And any simplistic model of anyone is cracked asunder by better acquaintance with the person. Artists put their imaginations to work to open our eyes to the realities that have been brushed away in the handling of abstractions. The voracious media tell personal stories and bring to the fore the realities neglected by the predominantly abstractive process of knowing that is best suited to verbal expression. Now images dominate, now complexity demands to be respected. Speed increases the density of the store of impressions. Everyone can be high by just letting life affect him, no need for drugs. Everyone can find endless resources in himself, even if "disabled," "handicapped," "socially underprivileged."

Indeed, the discovery of today is that <u>our</u> clumsiness, <u>our</u> amateurishness in some areas, <u>our</u> slowness at learning where to put our energies, the energies of the self, <u>our</u> neglect of what matters, <u>our</u> concentration on what the past believed to be true, <u>our</u> carelessness, all are the causes of our present dire conditions. It is not for nothing that present-day people everywhere have discovered that education, a functional education, is needed for all of us to work together to set our house, Earth, in order. A "true" education always seems the preliminary to any new movement in any sphere of human action.

What we have to learn, and learn all the time, is how to become more human. The meaning of this is that we have to make transcendence an instrument of every involvement, and acknowledge that, in addition to giving the time of our life to some experience, we have to use our awareness of our self within the experience to find that our experience does not exhaust all that is possible then and there. By leaving all doors open all the time, as we all do spontaneously in our early childhood, we see all our learnings as renewing and renewable in order to become more ourselves.

Although all the learnings we have considered in the earlier chapters are human learnings, there is still need of one more human learning—learning about being human. Although it is true that language distinguishes man from the animals, it is just as true that thinking new thoughts, building roads, traveling by sea, air, rail, creating economies, and so on, are equally good for that purpose. In mankind we also have realities that are capable of distinguishing between man and man, and they have been used throughout history to make the objectification of some ideas possible, when men's energies were muscular (in work), were intellectual (in government), were social (in economics). All these distinction have created groups that we may call "pre-human." They still persist today, but are on the way out, to be replaced by individual persons, or "humans," who are striving to eliminate in all activities, at all levels, the superimposed distinctions that reduce the spectrum of manifestation of every one of us.

Pre-humans remain pre-human because their selves adhere to one or more of the objectifications they have produced, although they do not see this adherence. When they do see what has happened, they can reduce their adherence, recuperate their energy, and become more themselves in that area. Once they have discovered that this movement is human, and can be used as often as they want in all the areas of living in which they find themselves, they have given themselves the impetus to become human. If adherence is never allowed to develop, because of the alertness of the educative environment on top of the self's own alertness, we shall have human education instead of the re-education of the pre-human. This is not an idea: it is the extension to each and every one of us of that which has been possible for some, and which they found to be an attribute of their selves and not due to chance.

From every place on Earth springs the affirmation that mankind is not an idea, that each of us can use all the endowments of the self to find, in alive life, all the ages of oneself functionally present and in any community all the generations that made it, accounting for all one's personal and cultural past. But through the act of transcendence, each finds the past, his past, as only one of the possible lives that could have been given to the self, and can move towards being available to the one that is coming. Unknown in actuality, its indeterminacy liberates the self to consider the future as the field of realizing itself. For this, only a state of suspended judgment is required, concomitant with every involvement of every moment, so that no expectations impose a mortgage upon what comes. Such a flexible state is human and makes it possible for us to find ourselves in a humanity that transcends societies, groups, communities, though formed of concrete persons each living through the four realms but specially given to the fourth through their consciousness.

As we have transcended all of the past by giving it its rightful place as a set of instruments devised to realize more of our selves, we have maintained both complexity in our lives and freedom for the self to use itself for human ends as it did in the prenatal period, the early period of childhood, and after that in some areas for many of us, and in many areas for some. As we have understood that transcendence is the human process <u>par excellence</u> for maintaining the self's contact with the future, we can see that we can actually place in our own hands the process of evolution and produce through a human education the humanity to which we belong by the mere fact of being Earthians.

The details of that education can be made explicit (and my work of the last forty or so years is available as one example of how transcendence can be kept at the center of our activities). The education of awareness, the only education that takes into account the self in all its involvements, is also today the only education that is illumined by the work of transcendence, for it shows the learners what they are doing with awareness at the same time as it shows them what they could do with it. The future remains open since the present is never circumscribed and the past is used only instrumentally. Memory is not invoked, retention is the result of functionings, know-hows are new functionings, and the self is made vulnerable to what comes.

Thus one finds that all that men have done with themselves can be done by everyone who is prepared to pay the price in time, concentration, dedication, and surrender. If the future is to remain true to what mankind has achieved—the extension of man's awareness and the movement towards knowing himself for what he can be—and is to preserve the variety that tells the story of mankind, the capacity of the intellect must be increased, the number of deliberately functionings sensitivities must be increased, the grasp of the various universes of expression must be increased, while the values that belong with an expanding self must be connected to it.

Values that assert a hierarchy of functions (other than the temporal hierarchies) cannot hold any more, since retention, intelligence, sensitivity, can all be made to work together and enrich each other. Values that state that a commitment to reason, or faith, or sentiment, is to be preferred above other commitments, cannot be upheld, since each is a particular instrument of the self that can peacefully co-exist and assist the others in their specific fields. Values that contrast the individual and the community need no longer be held because now we can see the community as made of individuals, the one serving the other in complementary ways. Values that discriminate between religions will also go, as religions can now be seen as the forms of being of men who relate to the whole through symbolisms which are historically and locally justified but do not conflict with each other at the level of the self.

A human education must be the education of an evolving man, always incomplete as to the future, always complete as to this moment and the past, always knowing that there is no conflict between living the here-and-now with all he is and becoming more himself as living reveals more and more of himself and the cosmos.

Thinking of the evolving self is equivalent to being in contact with the whole, the whole that intuition can grasp, for which intuition has been created—which all of us own. When we all know how to use it, the era of intuition, as the way of knowing the whole and maintaining the self in contact with the whole, will be with us—in the way that the uses of perception and action are with all of us today as ways of knowing and the use of the intellect as a way to know the world and of affectivity as a way to know feelings are with almost all of us.

Still, the evolving self does not place a ceiling on its ways of knowing, and the future may produce men and women (or some new being) who, taking as a springboard all that has been and is available today, will reach further manifestations of the self in a universe permeated by man's spirit.

In that human universe a person knowing himself will live a human life, hold human values, and look at the past as we do at the rest of Creation—amazed by what we find, fascinated by what we comprehend but full of respect for what we see, ourselves pursuing our pre-human lives.

# Further Readings by Caleb Gattegno

These publications are available from Educational Solutions, 95 University Place, New York, NY 10003-4555.

On Being Freer

The Universe of Babies

The Adolescent and His Will

Know Your Children As They Are (composed of material from The Universe of Babies, Of Boys and Girls, and the Adolescent and His Will)

Un Nouveau Phenomene Psychosomatique

Conscience de la Conscience

*III*
*The Mind Always Educates the Brain*

Towards a Visual Culture

The Silent Way (of teaching foreign languages)

The Scientific Study of the Problems of Reading

The Common Sense of Teaching Mathematics

The Common Sense of Teaching the Deaf

What We Owe Children

Gattegno Mathematics

For the Teaching of Mathematics

www.ingramcontent.com/pod-product-compliance
Lightning Source LLC
Chambersburg PA
CBHW081800300426
44116CB00014B/2188